Amazing Chesed

Living a Grace-Filled Judaism

Rabbi Rami Shapiro

EasyRead Large

Copyright Page from the Original Book

Amazing Chesed:
Living a Grace-Filled Judaism

2013 First Digital Edition

For information regarding permission to reprint material from this book, please mail or fax your request in writing to Jewish Lights Publishing, Permission Department, at the address / fax number listed below, or e-mail your request to permissions@jewishlights.com.

Library of Congress Cataloging-in-Publication Data
Shapiro, Rami M.
Amazing chesed : living a grace-filled Judaism / Rabbi Rami Shapiro.
pages cm.
Includes bibliographical references.
ISBN 978-1-58023-624-9
1. God (Judaism)—Love. 2. Grace (Theology) 3. Bible. O.T.—Theology. I. Title.
BM610.S474 2013
296.3'114—dc23
2012039482

10 9 8 7 6 5 4 3 2 1

Manufactured in the United States of America

Cover Design: Jenny Buono
Cover art: ©iStockphoto.com/Alex Sava

Published by Jewish Lights Publishing
A Division of LongHill Partners, Inc.
Sunset Farm Offices, Route 4, P.O. Box 237
Woodstock, VT 05091
Tel: (802) 457-4000 Fax: (802) 457-4004
www.jewishlights.com

ReadHowYouWant partners with publishers to provide books for ALL Kinds of Readers. For more information about Becoming A **RHYW** Registered Reader and to find more titles in your preferred format, visit:
www.readhowyouwant.com

TABLE OF CONTENTS

Preface

This book rests on three assumptions:

1. In the teaching of Judaism, grace is often over-looked.
2. In the living of Judaism, grace is, for many Jews, a lost virtue.
3. Without a sophisticated knowledge of grace as Judaism understands grace, Jews are robbed of an important component of their faith that leaves them with only a partial understanding of their tradition, their God, and the life they are called to live.

I came to these assumptions through my experience teaching a course at Middle Tennessee State University called "Judaism, Christianity, and Islam." Early in each semester I ask students to identify concepts central to each of the three religions we are examining. The idea of grace, the infinite, unconditioned, and unconditional love of God for all reality, is almost always among them.

My Muslim students point out the centrality of grace in Islam and cite the *Bismillah* as proof: bismi-lla-hi r-rah.ma-ni r-rah.i-m, "In the name of Allah [God] the Most Gracious, the Most Merciful." This phrase is recited before reading any *sura* (chapter) of the Qur'an.

My Christian students also claim grace as central to their faith, often citing Saint Paul's Letter to the Romans, "You are not under law but under grace"

(Romans 6:14), and John's Gospel, "The law indeed was given through Moses; grace and truth came through Jesus Christ" (Gospel according to John 1:17), as their proof texts.

My Jewish students—and I must admit these have been few in number—have yet to link Judaism with grace; justice is their concept of choice, and Deuteronomy 16:20 is their preferred text: "Justice, justice shall you pursue." While I, too, am partial to justice and proud that justice is so central to my people and our religion, I am saddened when Jewish students dismiss grace as a valid and vital aspect of Judaism. Here is a selection from a paper written for my class by a Jewish student:

> Grace is central to Christianity but not Judaism, from which Christianity derives. Indeed, the focus on grace may be one of the essential dividing points separating Judaism and Christianity. In Romans 11:6 St. Paul writes, "There is at the present time a remnant [of true believers] chosen by grace. And if it is by grace [that they are chosen] it is no longer on the basis of works, otherwise grace would no longer be grace."
>
> Judaism is the exact opposite of this. When offered the Ten Commandments by God on Mount Sinai the people responded, "*Naaseh v'nishma,* we will do and then we will understand" (Exodus 24:7), implying that works trump faith, belief, and even grace. (Used with permission)

While Judaism and certain branches of Protestant Christianity may differ on the issue of grace versus works, what troubles me is this student's blanket dismissal of grace as central to Judaism. When I asked her about this, she told me that her position was informed by what she learned from her rabbis and lay teachers. Over her years of Sunday school and Bat Mitzvah training, she was taught that grace was Christian, and works was Jewish; that faith was Christian, and works was Jewish; that believing was Christian, and doing was Jewish; and that love was Christian, and law was Jewish. In essence she was taught by her rabbis to view Judaism through a Christian, and more specifically Pauline, lens:

> Gentiles who didn't strive for righteousness [through the law] have yet attained it through faith; but Israel, who did strive for righteousness through the law, failed to fulfill that law, and hence did not attain righteousness. Why did they fail to attain righteousness? Because they strove for it based on works and did not strive for it based on faith. They have stumbled over the stumbling block. (Romans 9:30–32)

> Brothers and sisters, I pray to God with all my heart that [the Jews] might be saved. I can testify to their passion for God, but it is a passion rooted in ignorance. They are ignorant of the righteousness that comes from God, and seek to establish their own [through the law], and in so doing have not surrendered to God's

righteousness. For with Christ the law ceases in order that righteousness be given to everyone who believes. (Romans 10:1–4)

According to Paul, righteousness, being in proper relationship with God, cannot be earned; it is a gift of grace that comes through faith in the salvific nature of the death and resurrection of Jesus as Christ. Doing *mitzvot* (God's commandments) and adhering to the rules set forth in Torah is impossible, for the legal standard set by God is purposefully set too high. Torah, as Paul understands it, is given to the Jews by God to show us the impossibility of living in accordance with divine command and to thereby prepare us to accept the grace of God that comes when we abdicate doing *mitzvot* for believing in Jesus as messiah.

Ironically, it may be that so few Jews know God's grace to be central to Judaism because too many Jews have been taught by teachers who seek to differentiate Judaism from Christianity and who use Paul's idea of grace versus works as a means for doing so. These teachers have, again following Paul, ceded grace to Christianity, allowed the idea of grace to fade from Judaism, and turned Judaism into a religion of works. The aim of this book is to correct the imbalance that this effort caused and to reclaim grace as a core Jewish idea not in opposition to works, but as a key for unlocking our understanding of the spiritual nature of the work we do.

This is not an encyclopedic effort: I'm not going to list every time a Jewish text or teacher speaks of God's grace. Rather I'm going to examine elements of Judaism in relation to grace so that you can see what our sages have seen—God's grace permeating all reality—and in so doing show how Judaism offers you a way to live graciously. Here too I'm not opting for the encyclopedic and won't read each of the 613 *mitzvot* of Judaism in light of grace. Instead I will highlight the role of grace in key aspects of Jewish practice, such as forgiveness, the Ten Sayings, and Shabbat, and do so in a way that will allow you to apply the lens of grace as you explore other aspects of Judaism on your own. In short, what this book will do is enrich your appreciation of grace in a Jewish context and deepen your appreciation of Judaism as a way of living graciously.

The impetus for this book came from Stuart M. Matlins, editor in chief, founder, and publisher of Jewish Lights Publishing. It was Stuart who helped me see the need for this book and who encouraged me to write it. But writing it and writing it well are two different things. That is where Emily Wichland, my longtime editor at both Jewish Lights and SkyLight Paths, comes in. Her skill at massaging a manuscript into a compelling text has served me well through ten prior books. I am grateful for, and indebted to, them both. I also wish to thank my son, Aaron, who, as my first reader, drew upon his critical skills as a professor of English to find the holes in my argument and to help me fill them.

Given the focus of this book, we will be drawing upon a lot of Hebrew and Aramaic texts. Unless otherwise stated, all translations are my own.

I hope you find this book of value to you as you strive to live grace-filled lives marked by good, just, and compassionate works.

Introduction

What Is Grace?

The word that will occupy us in the chapters that follow is *chesed.* Often translated into English as "love" or "loving-kindness," *chesed* is better understood as "grace," which, following the work of Yudit Greenberg[1] and Rabbi Lawrence A. Hoffman,[2] I define as *God's unlimited, unconditional, unconditioned, and all-inclusive love for all creation.*

It is crucial that you grasp the implications of this definition. Everything else in this book revolves around it, and the ideas we will explore will be incomprehensible without it. So let's go into this definition slowly, one word at a time.

To say that God's grace is *unlimited* is to say that there is no one outside its reach. No one: not the sinner, the heretic, the unbeliever, or the differently believing believer. No one. While one faith group or another may claim to have a monopoly on God's grace, this is mere marketing and in no way reflects the truth of God's unlimited grace.

To say that God's grace is *unconditional* is to say that there is nothing one can do to merit grace, earn grace, or even avoid grace. Neither doing *mitzvot* nor affirming a specific creed will bring you closer to God's grace. You cannot get closer or further away from grace; grace is unlimited and all-encompassing. It is "here" and "there" and everywhere in between. Similarly, you cannot get more or less grace; you can only get all of grace. *Chesed* is free, and there are no conditions placed upon it at all. I mean this absolutely: the sinner no less than the saint receives the entirety of God's grace. This is what it means to say *chesed* is unconditioned: you cannot earn it, and you cannot escape it. The difference between sinner and saint isn't the quality or quantity of grace they receive, but what they do with what they get.

To say that God's grace is *unconditioned* is to say that *chesed* is not restricted by human notions of good and bad, just and unjust, the desirable and the undesirable. *Chesed* is the fullness of God's infinite love bestowed without filters upon all creation. Job understands this when he says to his wife, "Shall we not accept the good as well as the bad from God?" (Job 2:10). Everything is from God, and grace is this everything. Sometimes it manifests in ways you might call "good," and sometimes it manifests in ways you might call "bad," but do not think God or God's grace is in any way limited to these or any categories.

Think in terms of the sun and sunlight. There are times when sunlight heals and times when sunlight kills; times when sunlight illumines and times when sunlight blinds; times when sunlight warms and times when sunlight burns. The sun doesn't decide when to shine one way and when to shine another. It doesn't decide who will warm and who will burn; it just shines. What we do with the sunlight we receive is up to us. Receiving it is not.

When we say God's grace is *all-inclusive,* we mean to summarize and emphasize the points just made: *Chesed* includes everyone and everything. There is no one who is left out of God's grace, and no thing that does not come from God's grace. Grace is what is, and what is is all that is and, over time, all that can be.

When we say *love,* please don't imagine a romantic love or even a contractual love. The love we are talking about isn't *quid pro quo,* "this for that." God's love isn't earned or merited; it is just given. But what is given isn't always what is desired. God's love reflects God's reality, and God's reality includes everything and its opposite. If we imagine God's love in human terms and expect it to be tender and affectionate, we will be sorely troubled when bad things happen to good people. When we realize that God is beyond human categories and that God's love is not analogous to human love; when we realize that God is the source of light and dark, good and evil (Isaiah 45:7), and that God's love is simply the bestowing of all this upon each of us, we will, as Job does, give thanks for both the blessings and the curses that come our way.

God's love, then, is not to be likened to human love. To what can it be likened? Again I opt for the metaphor of the sun and sunlight. God is the sun, and sunlight is God's grace. God graces us the way the sun shines upon us. Just as the sun doesn't choose to shine, so God doesn't choose to be gracious. Just as the sun doesn't choose upon whom it will shine, so God doesn't choose upon whom to be gracious. Just as sunlight from the human perspective can be experienced as both positive and negative while being neither in and of itself, so God's grace from the human perspective can be positive and negative while being neither in and of itself. This is absolute love understood as the bestowing of the totality of reality on each of us. If, as I was once told, love is about giving unto others what they would like to receive, God's love is giving unto others everything that can be received whether they would like to receive it or not.

Chesed isn't a reward; it is reality. God's grace isn't limited to what we want to happen or might like to happen. God's grace is what is happening whether we like it or not. In short, God's grace is the giving of all to all.

This way of understanding grace draws upon the kabbalistic notion that *alles iz Gott,* that all is God. God is the sole Reality, the source and substance of all things. There is nothing outside of God, for if there were, then God would no longer be infinite, and a finite God isn't the God of Judaism. Thus Torah says, "I am *YHVH* and there is none else" (Isaiah 45:5). Not simply that there is no other god but *YHVH,* but that there is nothing else but *YHVH.* Similarly when Torah says, "*YHVH* alone is God in heaven above and on earth below; there is none else" (Deuteronomy 4:39), the notion of *ein od*—none else—means that there is nothing else in heaven or on earth but God.

God is the infinite source of existence. God is that from whom and in whom all things rise and to whom and in whom all things return, and grace is this rising and returning: existence itself as each of us experiences it. You cannot control existence; all you can do is learn to work with it, to navigate God's grace in such a way as to live graciously with a sense of radical acceptance, abounding compassion, and deep tranquility.

This is where Judaism as a spiritual practice comes in. When grace is seen as essential to life, Judaism becomes a way to live graciously. *Mitzvot* are no longer means of pleasing God or earning rewards in this life or some other, but the means for working with the grace of God in ways that benefit life and the living. Jewish holy days are no longer just expressions of our history, but vehicles for navigating the grace of God in a manner that brings us into ever more mindful and compassionate relation with the life within us and the lives around us.

In the chapters that follow, we will take up some of the hallmarks of Jewish thought and practice and see what they have to say about *chesed* and how our understanding of *chesed* as God's unlimited, unconditional, unconditioned, and all-inclusive love for all creation can deepen our appreciation for and engagement with Judaism.

Part One

The Theory of Grace

Chapter 1

Grace & God

If we are to understand God's grace, we must understand God—not God in and of God's own self, for that is beyond us, but God as we understand God. Because theological speculation is human rather than divine in origin, theology tells us more about the theologian than about God. The limitations of theology are the limitations of theologians, which is why, for example, a Christian theologian will never come to the conclusion that Krishna rather than Christ is the Second Person of the Holy Trinity, or that the Qur'an rather than the Bible is the final and uncorrupted word of God. Theologians set out to prove their assumptions rather than challenge them. This is no less true of me than it is of any other theologian. The God I discover at the end of my speculation is the God I start with at the beginning. So let me be clear: what follows isn't the only way to think about God and grace, just the only way I can think about God and grace.

The One and Only

At the heart of my understanding of God is the as yet unshakable notion that God is one. I understand this not only in the numerological sense that there is one God rather than three or three thousand Gods, but in the sense that there is but one unbroken and unbreakable living system that embraces and transcends the universe in all its glory. God isn't just one, but the one and only.

God, for me, isn't a being or even a Supreme Being, but be- *ing* itself. God is the source and substance of all reality. God is what is, what was, what will be, and what could ever be. God is both the diversity of the manifest world—the world that you and I experience through our senses and the technologies we use to enhance them—and the infinite possibility of worlds we cannot even imagine.

YHVH: The Happening One

Is this view of God a legitimately Jewish view? I think so, and I am far from the first to say so. Let's begin with Moses's encounter with God at the Burning Bush. Charged with returning to Egypt to free the enslaved Israelites, Moses asks God's name in hopes of using the name to authenticate his encounter with God and thus earn the trust of the Israelites he plans to lead.

Moses asked God, "When I say to the Israelites, 'The God of your ancestors has sent me to you,' they will ask me, 'What's God's name?' How shall I answer them?" God replied, *"Ehyeh asher Ehyeh.* Tell the Israelites that *'Ehyeh* has sent me to you.' Say to them, *'YHVH,* the God of your ancestors, the God of Abraham, the God of Isaac, and the God of Jacob, has sent me to you.' This shall be My name forever. This shall be My name for all eternity."

(EXODUS 3:13–15)

While the four-letter name of God, *YHVH,* has already been used throughout Genesis and is not new to the Torah as a whole, this is the first and only time the name is unwrapped as *Ehyeh asher Ehyeh.* When God encounters Abraham, God says, "I am *El Shaddai.* Walk in My ways and be guiltless" (Genesis 17:1). God refers to this encounter when speaking to Moses after their encounter at the Bush: "I appeared to Abraham, Isaac, and Jacob as *El Shaddai,* but I didn't make Myself known to them by my name *YHVH"* (Exodus 6:3).

El Shaddai may mean "God of the High Place," or "Mountain God." The Israelites may have borrowed the name from the Mesopotamians, whose God was called *El Shaddai,* or they may have adapted it later when looking for a name that would link God to Mount Sinai. Or *El Shaddai* may be the "Breasted God" *(shad* and *shadayim* being the Hebrew words for "breast" and "breasts," respectively), referring to a life-giving

God of fertility. In any case, Exodus clearly links *El Shaddai* with *YHVH,* and *YHVH* with *Ehyeh asher Ehyeh.*

To understand the connection, we must unpack the meaning of *Ehyeh asher Ehyeh* and *YHVH.* We are so accustomed to the translation of the first name of God as "I am what I am" that we may miss the fact that *Ehyeh* is dynamic rather than static, a verb rather than a noun. *Ehyeh* is the first-person singular imperfect form of the Hebrew verb *hayah,* "to be." *Ehyeh* isn't "I am," but "I will be" or "I am becoming" or even "I am- *ing."* God isn't fixed, but flowing; God isn't the unmoved mover, but the ever-moving is- *ing* of reality. In effect what God says to Moses at the Burning Bush is this: My name, My nature, is be *ing,* happen *ing,* creat *ing,* caus *ing,* manifest *ing,* is -*ing.*

The unpronounceable name, the Tetragrammaton, *YHVH,* is also a verb and is also drawn from the Hebrew *hayah,* "to be," and its variant *havah.* Adding the *y* (the Hebrew letter *yod)* to the beginning of the word renders *hayah* in the causative *(hif'il)* and yields the meaning "causing existence to be" or "giving life." With these meanings in mind we can see how *El Shaddai* fits in. If *El Shaddai* is the Breasted God, the nursing God, the God who gives life, then *El Shaddai* is also *YHVH* and *Ehyeh,* the life-giving One.

So in the context of our exploration of grace, don't imagine God as a being or even a Supreme Being somewhere outside of time or space (there can be no "somewhere" outside time and space, since the very idea of "outside" and "somewhere" implies space), but rather imagine God to be be- *ing* itself manifesting time, space, and everything that occupies them. God isn't a noun but a verb; God isn't a being but a doing, and what God does is called grace.

Our Mystics Speak

While this idea of God may be new to you, and even a bit troubling, it is a constant that runs through much of Jewish mystical thought. Rabbi Moshe Cordovero (1522–1570), for example, one of the most famous teachers of the Zohar, the thirteenth-century "bible" of Jewish mysticism, put it this way:

> [God] is found in all things and all things are found in God, and there is nothing devoid of divinity, heaven forfend. Everything is in God, and God is in everything and beyond everything, and there is nothing beside God.[1]

Rabbi Schneur Zalman of Liadi (1745–1812), the founder of Chabad Hasidism, taught something similar some two hundred years later: "Everything is God, blessed be He, who makes everything be and in truth the world of seemingly separate entities is entirely annulled."[2] And two hundred years after Schneur Zalman, Rabbi Menachem Mendel Schneerson (1902–1994) continues the teaching, saying:

> The absolute reality of God, while extending beyond the conceptual borders of "existence," also fills the entire expanse of existence as we know it. There is no space possible for any other exis-

tences or realities we may identify—the objects in our physical universe, the metaphysical truths we contemplate, our very selves ... do not exist in their own reality; they exist only as an extension of divine energy....[3]

All of this may be summed up in the most central teaching of Judaism, the *Shema:* "Hear, O Israel, *YHVH* is our God, *YHVH* is one" (Deuteronomy 6:4). The conventional reading of this text is numerical: there is only one God and not more than one God. But Jewish mystics have always read more into this teaching than arithmetic. The Baal Shem Tov, the eighteenth-century founder of Hasidic Judaism, taught, "The phrase '*YHVH* is One' means nothing other than God permeates all existence."[4] Sfat Emet, a nineteenth-century Hasidic sage (1847–1905), said, "The meaning of '*[YHVH]* is One' is not that [God] is the only God negating all other gods ... [but that] there is no being other than [God], even though it seems otherwise to most people."[5]

Second only to the *Shema* as proof for God's nonduality is Deuteronomy 4:35, "*YHVH* is God; there is none else." Again the conventional reading is numerical, but Jewish mystics read it philosophically: the phrase "none else" *(ein od)* is read not as "no other god beside God," but as "there is no other reality other than God." As Rabbi Isaiah HaLevy Horowitz (1565–1630) taught, "Not just no other god beside God, but nothing exists except God."[6]

Promoting the same idea from yet another text of Torah, in this case Isaiah 6:3, "The whole earth is filled with Divine Glory," Rabbi Menachem Nahum of Chernobyl (1730–1797) taught, "The whole earth is filled with this [divine] presence; there is no place devoid of it. There is nothing besides the presence of God; being itself is derived from God and the presence of the Creator remains in each created thing."[7] He also wrote:

> All is one: God, Israel, Torah, the world-to-come, and this world. All bring forth the flow of Godliness, this world in a more external way, but containing within it that inward self of the world-to-come. These must be joined into a total one-ness, such that all will allow body to be translated into soul, just as happens with a single human person.[8]

Rabbi Meshullam Feibush Heller of Zbarazh, a contemporary of Menachem Nahum, wrote something similar:

> There is really nothing in the world other than God and God's emanated powers which are a unity. Other than that, nothing exists. Although it seems that there are other things, everything is really God and the divine emanations.[9]

So for us, backed by Torah and some of its greatest teachers, God is reality—seen and unseen, known and unknown, and, in part, even unknowable. Given this definition, how then shall we define grace?

Grace Defined

In the introduction to this book I defined grace as *God's unlimited, unconditional, unconditioned, and all-inclusive love for all creation.* With the added input of these Jewish sages I would amend the definition slightly: *Chesed,* grace, is *God's unlimited, unconditional, unconditioned, and all-inclusive love for all creation manifesting in and as all reality.* In other words, if God is doing, grace is what God does.

As with our definition of God, our definition of grace may be troubling. We are used to thinking of grace as reward and the absence of grace as punishment or at least indifference. But *YHVH,* be- *ing* itself, doesn't reward and punish; *YHVH* simply does, and what *YHVH* does sometimes works in our favor and sometimes doesn't. But *YHVH* sets out to do neither. God is what is:

> From east to west, there is none but Me. I am *YHVH* and there is nothing else. I form light and create darkness, I make good and create evil—I, *YHVH,* do all this.
>
> (ISAIAH 45:6–7)

While we may like some of what *YHVH* does and dislike some of what *YHVH* does, the doing itself is *YHVH,* and what is done, like it or not, is grace.

God is light and dark, good and evil, and cannot be otherwise. If we say that God is good only, then

God is limited to the good. And not only that: God is limited to good as we define good. If we then limit grace to what is good as we define good, we have made humans rather than God the arbiter of grace. But God, at least as we understand God in this book, is everything and its opposite, and that which embraces and transcends both. And grace is the manifestation of God's be- *ing* and hence no less a play of opposites.

An apt metaphor for God is a magnet. A magnet has a positive pole and a negative pole and cannot be a magnet without them. The two poles cannot be separated one from the other: you cannot slice a magnet in two and have a positive magnet and a negative magnet. Yet the magnet is more than either pole or even both poles together. A magnet is that which embraces the two poles in something larger, but this something larger cannot be separated from that which it embraces. You cannot remove the poles of a magnet and still have something called a magnet. So, as with God, a magnet is not really a noun or a thing, but a happening. A magnet happens when positive and negative poles are held together in a seamless and yet dynamic tension. Think of the poles as the grace of God, positive and negative from our perspective. God "happens" as grace happens, for "gracing" is what God's be- *ing* is all about.

God includes all polarity: good and evil, light and dark, in and out, up and down, front and back, self and other. God is not limited to these opposites, but like the magnet and its poles, God is not God without them. And, again like a magnet, the poles—you, me, and the entirety of existence—cannot be separated from each other or the Greater Whole, God, who holds and manifests them.

In the Rabbinic literature of the early sages, the polarity of God was commonplace. Indeed "there is scarcely a passage which refers to [God's] capacity as Judge which does not also allude to His attribute of compassion."[10] In fact the early Rabbis taught that the Hebrew compound name of God, *YHVH Elohim,* refers to the mixture of justice and *chesed* within God. *Elohim,* they taught, referred to the divine attribute of *din,* justice, and *YHVH* referred to the divine attribute of *chesed,* understood in this case as mercy:

> This may be likened to a king who had empty vessels he wanted to fill. He said to himself, "If I fill them with boiling water they will expand and crack, and if I fill them with icy water they will contract and crack." What did the king do? He mixed the boiling water with icy water and filled the vessels with the mixture, and in this way the vessels survived. It is the same with God. The Holy One said, "If I create the world with *chesed* alone, sin will abound, but if I create the world with justice alone, it will be condemned. So I shall create the world with both and in so doing ensure its survival."

(GENESIS RABBAH 12:15)

While we are taking *chesed* to be something greater than mercy alone, exploring the Rabbis' more limited use of the term can help us see that the unity of opposites in God is a core Jewish teaching. Listen to what the Rabbis have to say in *Pirke Avot,* the first-century anthology of their ethical teachings:

> Why were there ten generations from Adam to Noah? To demonstrate God's patience, for each generation angered God, but it took the cumulative disappointment of all ten to bring on the Flood.

(PIRKE AVOT 5:2)

The Hebrew for "patience" here is *erech apayim,* literally "long *[erech]* noses *[apayim]."* The phrase reflects the fact that people flare their nostrils or scrunch up their nose when they get angry. God's nose remains long and straight, unaffected by anger, for God remains calm and unangered. But why the plural form *apayim* rather than the singular *af?* Does God have two noses? The Rabbis took the plural form to mean that God's grace extends to the righteous and the wicked alike (Talmud, *Baba Kamma* 50b): God's nose remains untroubled in the face of the righteous and untroubled in the face of the wicked.

The Rabbis are making midrash here: reading into the texts of Torah to find their own sensibility reflected in them. Torah, however, is less inclined to speak of God in terms of *chesed* than the Rabbis. Moses, for example, describes God as "great, mighty, and terrible" (Deuteronomy 10:17); the prophet Jeremiah calls God "great and mighty" (Jeremiah 32:18); and the prophet Daniel calls God "the great and terrible" (Daniel 9:4). But when the Rabbis speak of God they see not might but grace: "This is the greatest manifestation of divine power: that God subdues anger and has patience with the wicked" (Talmud, *Yoma* 69b).

To prove their grace-filled vision of God, the Rabbis resorted to basic arithmetic. In Exodus 20:5–6 we are told that God "visits the sins of the parents upon the children up to the third and fourth generations," but we are also told that God shows *chesed* "to thousands of generations." The Hebrew for thousand is *alafim,* plural, so the Rabbis said God's mercy must extend at least two thousand generations if not more. Based on this, they argued that God's anger lasts no more than four generations, while God's grace lasts at least two thousand generations, making God's *chesed* (grace) outweigh God's *din* (justice) by a factor of 500 to 1 *(Tosefta Sotah* 4:1).

But even this level of grace wasn't strong enough for the Rabbis. Anything other than grace is problematic when it comes to God. So the Rabbis taught that even when God appears angry, God's focus is on *chesed* (Talmud, *Pesach* 87b). At the moment of divine anger God prays that *chesed* will overcome justice: "May it be My will that My grace subdue My wrath; and may My grace prevail over My justice, so that I may deal with My children in the quality of grace rather than the strict line of justice" (Talmud, *Berachot* 7a).

God's grace is the strongest of the divine attributes as the Rabbis understood them: "Even if 999 angels testify against humanity and only 1 speaks on their behalf, the Holy One, blessed be, inclines the scales in humanity's favor" (Talmud, *Kiddushin* 61d).

Even in those cases when the wrath of God was undeniable, the Rabbis sought to soften it. In the story of the Exodus, for example, God drowns the army of Pharaoh in the Reed Sea, and as God does so, the Rabbis imagine the angels in heaven bursting into song. God silences them saying, "The work of My hands is drowned in the sea, and you would offer Me a song!" (Talmud, *Sanhedrin* 39b). While God was angry enough with the Egyptians to drown them in the sea, God was at the same time saddened by their deaths and refused any to celebrate it. So while it is true that God is called the Judge of the Universe, the Rabbis preferred the title *Rachmana* (the Compassionate One), saying, "The world is judged by grace" *(Pirke Avot* 3:19).

As noted in our preface, it is commonplace to juxtapose Judaism and Christianity by saying the former is all about works and the latter is all about grace, but Christianity is less a revolution than many Christians would have us believe, and the Rabbis before and after Jesus rested their worldview and theology in grace. Some manuscripts of *Pirke Avot* quote this teaching of Rabbi Akiva: "Everything is foreseen, yet freedom of choice is given. And the world is judged by grace, and not according to the amount of work."[11]

For the ancient Rabbis, God lives in a place of grace. In Psalm 68:5 we read, "Sing to God, sing praises to God's name, lift up a song to the One who rides upon the *aravot,* whose name is *YHVH,* be joyous before God." In most English translations of this psalm, *aravot* is rendered as "clouds," but our early sages understood it as a level of heaven "in which rest righteousness and grace, the treasures of life, the treasures of peace and bliss" (Talmud, *Chagigah* 12b).

Given that we are talking about rabbis, however, nothing is as simple as it seems.

A Roman matron confronted Rabbi Jose ben Chalafta: "Your God is a capricious God, drawing close whomsoever it pleases." Rabbi Jose offered the woman a basket of figs and invited her to eat. The woman examined the fruit and chose the best among them. He said to her, "When it comes to figs you naturally choose the best for yourself, and yet you assume God acts differently? Nonsense. God looks at us and chooses those who do good."

(NUMBERS RABBAH 3:2)

For Rabbi Jose, God's grace is not unconditional, but dependent on our behavior: the good are rewarded, the rest are rejected. His position was the minority opinion,[12] however. In the same Talmudic passage, Rabbi Nehemiah, speaking in the name of Rabbi Samuel ben Rabbi Isaac, spoke for the majority: "Not everyone God draws near stays near, and not everyone who is far from God stays far from God" *(Numbers Rabbah* 3:2). While subtle, the difference between these two views is crucial.

First, remember that grace is what God does just as sunlight is what the sun does. The sun doesn't draw you close or push you away. The sun shines on all equally. It is up to the individual whether to step into the light or avoid it by remaining in the dark. There are times, Rabbi Nehemiah seems to be saying, when people will prefer the light and times when they will prefer the dark. The decision is yours rather than God's. Second, unlike the sun, God is both light and dark. Even those who avoid the light cannot avoid God (who is everything and beyond everything) or God's grace, that is, the world as it presents itself to them at any given moment.

Rabbi Jose offers us a fixed system of God and grace, with the good receiving grace and moving closer to God, while the wicked receive no grace and move further away from God. Rabbi Nehemiah offers us a dynamic system of God and grace where people accept or reject grace, but God offers it unconditionally. In this book we prefer Rabbi Nehemiah to Rabbi Jose: God's grace is unconditional, but our acceptance of God's grace is not. God's grace is given the way the sun gives sunshine: to everyone regardless of merit. But there are those who refuse the gift of sunlight and stand only in the shadows. Or to borrow a different Rabbinic analogy, Torah is given to the world like rain *(Genesis Rabbah* 6:4), but some of us prefer to stay dry beneath an awning rather than become drenched in the grace of God.

What I am saying then is this: God is the is- *ing* of reality, and grace is what results from that is- *ing.* Since God is unconditioned, God's grace is unconditioned; because God is not limited to a certain set of conditions, God's grace cannot be limited to a certain set of conditions. Since God is unconditional; God's grace is unconditional; because God cannot be bribed, God's grace cannot be earned. Because you cannot earn grace, grace isn't a reward. A reward has to be earned, but God's grace is freely given whether you deserve it or not. But remember, God is reality, and God's grace is reality as you experience it, so please don't imagine that the grace you receive is always the grace you want.

Does God Choose?

Grace is the doing of God the way sunlight is the doing of the sun. Shining is what a sun does because it is the nature of a sun to shine. A sun that doesn't shine isn't a sun. Grace-ing is what God does because it is the nature of God to grace. A God that doesn't grace—that is, a God that doesn't manifest a world as the consequence of grace—isn't God. Neither God nor the sun has any choice in this. Neither can be other than it is.

This is sometimes difficult to grasp because we often misunderstand God's unconditionality as being synonymous with choice and then imagine that God is free to choose to be graceful and free to choose to be ungraceful. But this is not true; God cannot choose. God's grace flows from God's nature the way sunlight flows from the sun. Neither God nor the sun chooses.

Yes, I know we Jews say that God chose us from among all the people's of the earth (Deuteronomy 7:6), but this is a reflection of sociological self-definition common to tribal peoples around the globe, rather than a statement of serious theological reflection. We will deal with the grace-filled nature of *brit,* covenant, in chapter 4, but if we imagine that God chooses the way humans choose, we reduce God to a cosmic potentate, something far less than *YHVH,* the singular be- *ing* of reality.

Here are just two problems with a choosing God that I believe render the idea inoperable. First, if God can choose, God has to choose between options: God can choose "this" or God can choose "that." But if God is all, then there is no "this" or "that" with God; God is "this" *and* "that" *and* "the other." As we recite daily in the *Amidah* prayer, *Ein od milvado,* "There is nothing else but God." So from what pool of options is God to choose? Since no options outside of God can exist, we are reduced to saying God chooses to be God, which isn't really a choice at all.

Second, if God can choose, there must be a set of criteria by which God determines what to choose. The criteria, if they are to be more than divine whim and fancy, must exist outside of God and must be capable of limiting God by limiting God's choices to those options best fitting the criteria that determines divine choice. If this is true, then God is not free at all, but a slave to a set of criteria God didn't create. In short, there is something greater than God. And this is exactly what we see in the story of the destruction of Sodom in the book of Genesis.

A Moral God

The author of the story of Sodom tells us that it is God's intent to wipe out the entire population of the city as punishment for the misdeeds of some. God confides this plan to Abraham, who is appalled by it and who sets himself up as God's moral compass in hopes of dissuading God from what Abraham clearly sees as an immoral choice of action (Genesis 18:17–23).

> What if there are fifty innocents within the city; will You then annihilate the place and not pardon the guilty for the sake of the innocent? How could You do such a thing: slaughter the innocent along with the guilty? How could You do

that! Shouldn't the Judge of all the earth do justly?

(GENESIS 18:24–25)

Clearly Abraham believes that God has a choice regarding the destruction of Sodom, and the criteria for making that choice is justice. When Abraham says that the Judge of all the earth must be just, he is saying that as powerful as God may be, there is something more powerful still: justice. And not justice as some amorphous ideal, but justice as Abraham himself defines it. Abraham believes it is unjust to slaughter the innocent along with the guilty and insists that God acquiesce to his moral stance. Amazingly, God does so and agrees not to destroy Sodom if there are fifty decent human beings dwelling there.

Who is the real power in this story? Abraham! A choosing God must choose according to some standard, and in this story it is Abraham who sets the standard. Having won the major point that God can be reined in by human moral criteria, Abraham then goes on to fight for a more stringent set of criteria than that which he first proposed. God thought it was just to slaughter Sodom if there were only forty-nine righteous people in it; Abraham holds to a higher standard and bargains with God until they settle on ten as the minimum number of righteous people necessary to save the entire town.

You may have an even stricter standard, insisting, for example, that if even a single righteous person resides in Sodom the city must be spared because it is wrong to kill the innocent along with the guilty. This is a standard Abraham (or the author of the Sodom story) does not hold, and so God is allowed to kill the innocent along with the guilty if only nine or fewer righteous people can be found there, which is exactly what happens.

What's important here is this: First, if God can choose, God can choose unwisely and immorally. This is how the story opens and why Abraham objects to God's choice. Second, if God's choices are conditioned by some set of criteria, that criteria can be determined by people and imposed upon God. This is the great bargain Abraham strikes with God. And if God's morality depends on human morality, we have a God whose grace is a matter of reward and punishment, rewarding those we want to reward and punishing those we want to punish. God is demoted from the Creator of all life to the Concierge of some of the living. This is not the God we are dealing with in *Amazing Chesed.*

A Capricious God

As long as we insist on a choosing God—the God of Sodom—we have but two options when it comes to God's grace: either grace is limited to a set of preconditions (for example, justice as Abraham defines it), or grace is capricious and God's choosing to be gracious to some and not to others is based on nothing but divine whim.

If you believe in a choosing but limited God—a God who must conform to human categories of morality—you can cite as your proof text Abraham arguing with God over the fate of Sodom. If, on the other hand, you believe in a choosing God whose choices are unlimited by any rules or conditions and are therefore capricious, you too have a proof text: "I will be gracious to whom I will be gracious, and I will be merciful to whom I will be merciful" (Exodus 33:19). While we will examine this text from Exodus in a different context in a moment, it is fair to say that for those looking to hang a capricious God on a Torah hook, this text is a great find.

A capricious God can be gracious or ungracious, merciful or cruel, and which God chooses to be is based on nothing more than whimsy. God just does what God wants when God wants to do it. There is no rhyme or reason to God's actions. Such a God is unconditioned in the sense that there is nothing to constrain God's choice (as opposed to Abraham's God who is constrained by Abraham's sense of moral justice), but God is still forced to choose: Shall I be gracious today or ungracious today? And the criteria for making this choice is nothing more than divine whim.

If God feels like being gracious and merciful to you, God will be; if God isn't so inclined, God won't be. Unlike Abraham's God, this God is bound not by external criteria, but by internal mood. But like Abraham's God, this God, too, is not free. As long as God must choose, God is not free, for there has to be some criteria—external or internal, logical or emotional—that determines that choice. God as I understand God, and God as this book understands God, is free, and a free God cannot choose.

Perhaps the strongest voice in opposition to my approach to grace is that of Rabbi Abraham Joshua Heschel, one of the major voices in twentieth-century Judaism. But the disagreement between us may be less than one might think.

For example, in *God in Search of Man,* Rabbi Heschel cites the nineteenth-century Rabbi Eliezer of Tarnegrod, who wrote, "Miracles happen at all times. However, since they come to us not because we deserve to be saved but because of His great mercy and grace, they remain unnoticed. Only a generation that serves Him wholeheartedly is worthy of knowing the miracles that happen to it."[13]

I'm not all that prone to talk of miracles—breaks in the order of nature—but life itself can be spoken of as miraculous, and certainly both Rabbis Heschel and Eliezer are saying that these gifts of God cannot be merited or unmerited. What can be earned, they say, is our ability to be aware of them. I differ with them on this for two reasons. First, who among us can serve God "wholeheartedly"? Second, modern science is making us ever more aware of the miraculous nature of reality.

The real area of disagreement between Rabbi Heschel and me, however, is more fundamental. While I cannot find a clear definition of God in his books, the God he describes seems to be self-conscious and willful. God is a free agent doing what He wants when He wants (I use the male pronoun because that is how Rabbi Heschel refers to God). This God seems to have needs and desires. My God is not free in this sense and has neither needs nor desires.

Heschel writes, and I concur up to a point, that "in the depth of human thinking we all presuppose some ultimate reality which on the level of discursive thinking is crystallized into the concept of a power, a principle or a structure. This, then, is the order in our thinking and existence: The ultimate or God comes first and our reasoning about Him second."[14] Fair enough. I have a deep and unshakable sense of structure beneath the surface of life as I encounter it. I call this structure God. I do not reason my way to God, but reason about God after affirming (albeit without proof) God's existence.

In this, Rabbi Heschel and I are applying Gödel's Incompleteness Theorem to theology. According to philosopher and logician Kurt Gödel (1906–1978), in mathematics there are always going to be statements made regarding natural numbers that are true and yet unprovable. The same is true of theology. Every theological system rests on assertions that the theologian holds to be true but that cannot be proved or disproved. They are simply assertions that have to be accepted as true if the theology based on them is to make sense or have some importance outside the play of theology itself.

For example, most Christian theologians affirm but none can prove the Holy Trinity, and yet without the Trinity and Jesus as the Second Person in it (alongside God the Father and the Holy Spirit), the conclusions of Christian theologians have no consequence at all. The same is true with rabbis speculating about God. Unless you are willing to affirm Rabbi Heschel's God, both God's search for man and man's quest for God (to use the titles of two of his books) are irrelevant.

This is the missing step in Rabbi Heschel's notion that the "ultimate or God comes first and our reasoning about Him second." Somewhere in there we also need a definition of God. Rabbi Heschel speaks of God as supernatural Person with free will. I find the idea of a God with free will untenable. Rabbi Heschel's God seems to choose one people over others, reveal one set of books rather than others, and proclaim one strip of land as holier than others. My God does none of this. My understanding of God is reality itself, the deep structure and the surface manifestation. God for me is the source and substance of all reality whose grace is that reality.

A Choiceless God

I am not deaf to how paradoxical this sounds. But it sounds paradoxical only because we equate freedom with choice. God's freedom arises not from the ability to choose, but from the ability to be choiceless. Having to choose among options limits God to those options and the criteria used for discerning which is the best among them. Being free from choice allows God to simply be God: to manifest reality in all its diversity and complexity without limit.

God is free to be God only when the necessity to choose is removed from the equation. Again, this is the God revealed to us in Isaiah: "From east to west, there is none but Me. I am *YHVH* and there is nothing else. I form light and create darkness, I make good and create evil—I, *YHVH,* do all this" (Isaiah 45:6–7).

This is the God Job knows when he says to his wife at the death of their children and the loss of their wealth and Job's health, "Shall we not accept the good as well as the bad from God?" (Job 2:10). This is the God who embraces and transcends all opposites and who is unbound by any of them. This is the God who is free from the limitation of having to choose. This is not a capricious God who is gracious to some and ungracious to others, but a God who is gracious to all, but whose grace is not always beneficial from the human point of view.

Let's look at our Exodus text again: "I will be gracious to whom I will be gracious, and I will be merciful to whom I will be merciful" (Exodus 33:19). Since there is no criteria for determining who will benefit from God's grace and mercy, there is a legitimate argument to be made for God being capricious. And, since there is nothing we can do but endure a capricious God, there is no point in bothering with God at all. But this is not the only way to read this text.

Notice that when God says, "I will be gracious to whom I will be gracious, and I will be merciful to whom I will be merciful," God doesn't juxtapose grace and mercy with their opposites. That is to say, there is no need for us to assume, as I did above, that God is saying, "I will be merciful to whom I will be merciful and cruel to whom I will be cruel, and there is nothing you can do about it." On the contrary, God is saying, "Because I am not bound by conditions, My grace and mercy flow without constraint. You cannot expect Me to grace those you deem worthy of grace and to curse those you deem worthy of cursing. Your categories are not Mine; I have no limitations and neither does My grace or mercy." In other words, God isn't capricious at all. God's grace is bestowed upon everyone all the time. It is just that God's grace includes everything: blessing and curse, life and death, the good and the bad.

Grace Unbound

If God contains all things and their opposite, and grace is the exuberance of God manifesting as all things and their opposite, then God's grace isn't limited to that which is beneficial to life; grace is life itself and everything that life can experience. The ultimate grace of God is reality itself, and reality contains both light and dark, both good and evil.

If God's grace is unconditioned, there can be no condition under which it is dispensed or not dispensed. God bestows grace the way the sun bestows sunlight: it isn't a choice but a necessary expression of what God is. There is no sun that doesn't shine. Similarly there is no God that doesn't bestow grace. Bestowing grace is what it means to be God. Grace is God "god-ing." By way of illustration, take the story of Cain and Abel.

The Grace of Cain

The brothers Cain and Abel each worship God in his own way. Abel's worship is lauded; Cain's is not. While Rabbinic commentators do their best to find reasons for God's preferring Abel's offering to Cain's, Torah gives us no hint as to why God elevates one brother over the other. Again, is God being capricious? Is this what the story is telling us: do your best but don't expect it to count for anything in the eyes of God? Or is the story telling us that God's nature is such that acceptance and rejection are both part of God and hence both part of God's grace, and we must learn to deal with whichever comes our way? I opt for the latter.

Cain comes to hate his brother and murders him. God punishes Cain with exile, the greatest punishment the ancient Hebrews could imagine, for to be cut off from the land was to be cut off from the protection of the God associated with that land, and hence left to the mercy of strangers. Knowing that as a landless wanderer he will be treated by others the way he treated Abel, Cain cries out to God, "I cannot bear this punishment! You have driven me from the land and exiled me from Your Face. I shall be a fugitive and a nomad, and anyone who wishes me dead can kill me." Then God says to Cain, "No. Whoever kills you will suffer vengeance seven times over." And God places a mark on Cain warning off any who would seek to slay him (Genesis 4:13–15).

What was this mark? Torah doesn't say, and for our purposes it doesn't matter. What does matter is that God has mercy on Cain for no reason whatsoever. Cain didn't repent. He expresses no regret over his brother's death. In fact his only concern is for his own safety. So why does God spare his life and protect him? I suggest the answer is this: God's grace is un-conditional.

If we are to posit that grace is freely given, we must also posit that grace is free-flowing; anything else is capricious. There are only two ways to avoid the charge of capriciousness with regard to grace. Either we insist that grace is not freely given and hence subject to conditions that must be met, that is, that grace is an earned reward; or we insist that grace is not only freely given but free-flowing, that it is ever present, and there is nothing one need do to earn grace, but rather all we need do is open ourselves to receiving what is already given.

If we argue for the former and hold that grace is conditional, then we have two further choices to make:

either the conditions are conditions that we can meet, or the conditions are so difficult that they cannot be met. If the conditions can be met, then God's grace can and must be earned, and we have to abandon our notion that God's grace is free and unconditional. If the conditions cannot be met, then we are again left with the notion that God's grace is capricious: God grants grace to some and withholds it from others without any criteria for doing so at all.

The only way out of this conundrum is to posit that grace is unbound and free-flowing, that it is given to the just and the unjust, the deserving and the un-deserving, and that there is no need to earn God's grace because we already have God's grace.

Choose Life, Choose Grace

While it is true that God can't choose, it is also true that we humans can't avoid choosing. This is how the Bible puts it in the book of Deuteronomy:

I summon earth and sky to witness this day that I place before you living and dying, blessing and cursing. Now choose life that both you and your descendants may live.

(DEUTERONOMY 30:19)

Don't imagine that the choice God offers you is between living *or* dying, blessing *or* curse, for real life contains all of this. The choice you are offered is whether to accept life as it is (the bi-polar world of living and dying, blessings and curses) or retreat into an imaginary world of one-pole magnets and gods who give us only what we want.

If you are a person who makes the latter choice, and you have somehow read this far into this book, you might want to put the book down and read no further. You will get little from it, and what little you do get will only upset you. But if you are still reading, and you are strong enough to choose life with all it joys and suffering without hiding behind a theological veil of one-sided gods and one-pole magnets, and if you are looking for a way of living the fierce grace of God with an equally fierce graciousness of your own—read on.

The Only Choice We Have

What God is saying is this: "I place before you the fullness of My grace: reality as it is with all its birthing and dying and blessing and cursing. Choose to live graciously with the grace I give, and teach your children to do so as well." Choosing to live with fierce grace and graciousness is what the rest of this book is about.

God withholds nothing from us: life and death are both present; blessing and curse are equally given. It isn't that we get to choose between these opposites, but that we get to choose whether to live at all (and hence engage with these opposites) or flee from life and seek a faux reality where magnets can be positive only and gods can be bribed to do our bidding.

When we choose life, we choose blessing and curse, birth and death. When we choose something else, we still receive blessing and curse, birth and death, but we are surprised every time this happens.

God's grace, God's essence freely given, is the totality of life as you and I experience it. There is no hiding from it. Yes, God says, "Choose life" (Deuteronomy 30:19), but don't assume that choosing life is choosing blessing, and choosing blessing is choosing grace, and by so choosing you escape death, curse, and adversity. Choosing life means choosing life as it comes to you: sometimes as a blessing, other times as a curse. Choosing life doesn't mean avoiding death, for life and death arise together. Choosing life means engaging reality as it is—the free and free-flowing grace of God.

Chapter 2

Grace & Creation

In a beginning, when God created the heavens and the earth, the earth was wild and chaotic; darkness blanketed the surface of the sea, while God's wind churned the face of the waters. Then God said, "Let there be light"; and there was light.

(GENESIS 1:1–3)

How the world was created or shaped is familiar to any reader of Genesis, but why it was created remains a mystery. Genesis gives us no insight into God's motivation. Rabbinic commentators on creation took this fact as an invitation to create their own backstory. I, on the other hand, see the absence of motivation as a sign of God's grace. No reason is given because no reason is necessary; God creates for the same reason the sun shines: it is God's nature to do so. God's unconditional grace needs no motivation; indeed this is what it means when we say grace is unconditional. There is no reason for creation except God's intrinsic grace-filled creativity.

And It Was Good

Read through the entire creation story of Genesis 1 and you will find, as you undoubtedly know, the phrase "And God saw that it was good [*tov*]" repeated over and over again: verses 4, 10, 12, 18, 21, 25, 31. Interspersed between God's acts of creation and these affirmations of goodness is the phrase "And it was so": verses 7, 9, 11, 15, 24, 30. Together these three form a pattern: God creating, the narrator confirming that creation, and God affirming that the creation is *tov,* good.

The Hebrew *tov* in this case isn't a moral judgment but an affirmation of completeness. Torah is saying that each act of creation was sufficient unto itself: light doesn't require that anything else be created, the emergence of dry land in the midst of the sea doesn't require the creation of vegetation, vegetation doesn't require the creation of animals, and the animals don't require the creation of humanity. Each act of creation in Genesis 1 is complete in and of itself, and because it is, the subsequent act of creation is an unconditional act of divine grace.

To see what I'm getting at, read Genesis 1 in reverse order, starting with the creation of humanity and ending with the creation of light. Read this way you can see that each act of creation necessitates the next: humanity cannot survive without food, so the creation of humankind would necessitate the creation of animals; animals also need food, hence the creation of vegetation; vegetation requires land in which to root, so the creation of vegetation would necessitate the creation of the earth; and people, animals, and plants require sunlight, so their creation would require the creation of the sun, and so on. Genesis 1 read in its proper sequence, beginning with light and ending with humankind, offers us a very different story, one in which no act of creation requires the next act of creation, so that each act of creation can only be the free-flowing grace of God.

The grace-filled creation of Genesis 1 is made even clearer when compared with the creation story told in Genesis 2:

> This is the history of sky and earth from the time they were created. When the God *YHVH* made earth and sky, there was no vegetation on the earth and no herbs had sprouted from the ground, for the God *YHVH* had not yet brought rain to the earth, and there was not yet anyone to till the soil, but a stream arose from the ground and watered it, and then the God *YHVH* formed an earthling from the dust of the earth and breathed life into him through his nostrils, and the earthling came alive and the God *YHVH* planted a garden in Eden, to the east, and put the earthling God had formed there.

(GENESIS 2:4–8)

In this story the emergence of life is dependent on the creation of a human capable of maintaining it by working the soil. Torah tells us that there was no vegetation because there was neither rain to feed it nor human to cultivate it. While the author of Genesis 1 argues that each act of creation was *tov*—complete and sufficient unto itself—the author of Genesis 2 makes the exact opposite point: creation of life on earth is dependent on God fashioning an earthling from the earth.

Genesis 2, however, doesn't negate creation as an act of grace, since here, too, we are left without any reason for creation, and the lack of a reason is evidence of grace.

Creation as Grace

Any remaining doubt that grace and creation are a seamless happening should be put to rest by Psalm 136, in which each act of creation is coupled with the phrase *ki l'olam chasdo,* "for God's grace [*chasdo*] is unending."

Give thanks to *YHVH,* for God is good;
for God's grace is unending.
Give thanks to the God of gods;
for God's grace is unending.
Give thanks to the Lord of lords;
for God's grace is unending.

Who alone works great wonders;
for God's grace is unending.
Who through understanding made the sky;
for God's grace is unending.
Who stretched the earth out upon the waters;
for God's grace is unending.
Who made the great lights;
for God's grace is unending.
The sun to rule the day;
for God's grace is unending.
The moon and stars to rule over the night;
for God's grace is unending.

(PSALM 136:1–9)

Creation is an expression of God's unending and unconditional grace. Take a breath and you are breathing the grace of God. Cast your gaze on any plant, tree, animal, or human, and you are gazing upon the grace of God. All existence is an expression of God's grace, so it isn't surprising that grace is linked with abundance. The prophet Isaiah makes this linkage explicit:

I will recount the grace-filled acts of *YHVH*,
the praiseworthy acts of *YHVH*,
because of all that *YHVH* has done for us,
and the great favor to the house of Israel
that God has shown them according to God's
 compassion,

according to the abundance of God's unwavering grace.

(ISAIAH 63:7)

According to Isaiah, the relationship between God and Israel is marked by grace, not a limited and time-bound grace, but a boundless and timeless (unwavering) grace that is the very nature of God. Moses Maimonides, the great twelfth-century rabbi and philosopher, confirms Isaiah's understanding when he tells us that "the very existence of creation is an act of God's grace."[1]

The meaning of *chesed* is excess in whatever matter excess is practiced. In most cases, however, it is applied to excess in beneficence. Now it is known that beneficence includes two notions, one of them consisting in the exercise of beneficence toward one who has no right at all to claim this from you, and the other consisting in the exercise of beneficence toward one who deserves it, but in greater measure than he deserves it. In most cases the prophetic books use the word *chesed* in the sense of practicing beneficence toward one who has no right to claim this from you. Therefore every benefit that comes from God, may God be exalted, is called *chesed....* Hence this reality as a whole—I mean that God, may God be exalted, has brought it into being—is *chesed.* Thus it says: "The world is built up in *chesed*" (Psalm 89:3), the meaning of which is: the building-up of the world is *chesed.*[2]

The key element Maimonides brings to our understanding of grace is "excess." Grace is God's effervescence, God's overflowing nature. God is infinite and hence uncontainable, and the endless and eternal outpouring of God's nature is *chesed. Chesed* goes beyond the necessary, for *chesed,* like God, knows no bounds. There is no reason for creation outside of the nature of God's creativity. God doesn't choose to create; God is creativity and creation and the infinite *chesed* that makes these possible. All of this, as Maimonides wrote, is confirmed by Psalm 89:

> O *YHVH,* I will sing of Your *chesed* without
> ceasing.
> From generation to generation
> I will speak of Your faithfulness.
> I declare: The world is established *[boneh]*
> through *chesed;*
> Your faithfulness is as stable as the sky.

(PSALM 89:2–3)

The Psalmist links the Hebrew word *boneh,* "to build or establish," with *chesed,* grace. For Maimonides the link is this: God's grace is always about excess; that is, it has no limit, it is boundless. And because it is boundless, it spills over in unpredictable ways. Imagine you are filling a pot with water and continue filling the pot long after it's full. The water flows effortless over the sides of the pot. In some places it may pool up, in others it may continue to flow downward, and it will continue to do so as long as you keep pouring water into the already full pot.

Think of the water as *chesed.* Since God is without end, the flowing of *chesed* is without end, and hence the flow of possibility is without end. Some of that flow shifts from possibility to actuality, and some of that actuality is the world that you and I know. God didn't set out to create our world, nor is our world the sum of God's creation. God's *chesed* is infinite and timeless excess. The worlds it fashions and continues to fashion are innumerable. But do not imagine that once created any world becomes stable. Creativity is rooted in *tohu va'vohu,* the wild and chaotic nature of things revealed in Genesis 1:2. *Chesed* is this wildness, which is why it can manifest as good as well as evil, as light as well as darkness, as blessing as well as curse, and why things always turn into their opposite. Nothing is stable because God isn't stable and everything is God.

The Fabric of Nature and the Nature of Grace

Maimonides was influenced by the writings of Alexander of Aphrodisias, whose book *On the Principles of the All* Maimonides read in the Arabic translation of the Greek original. To understand Maimonides's position on grace, it is helpful to begin with Alexander of Aphrodisias:

> For the fabric of this universe and the natural grace dealt out by the Creator in the natural agreement and accord of its parts and in their being fashioned in [due] relation to the universe [as a whole] are such that if you should conceive the thought that one of these parts should be considered as abolished [it would mean] that none of them could remain as it is.[3]

In other words, the universe is a single system of interrelated parts, none of which can be separated from the others or from the whole that manifests them. The reason the world is so created is because of the grace of God. Here is how Maimonides, himself, put it:

> If you consider the divine actions—I mean to say the natural actions—the deity's wily graciousness and wisdom, as shown in the creation of living beings, in the gradations of the motions of the limbs, and the proximity of some of the latter to others, will through them become clear to you. Similarly His wisdom and wily graciousness, as shown in the gradual succession of the various states of the individual, will become clear to you.... Similarly the deity made a wily and gracious arrangement with regard to all the individuals of the living beings that suck. For when born, such individuals are extremely soft and cannot feed on dry food. Accordingly breasts were pre-

pared for them so that they should produce milk with a view to their receiving human food....[4]

In other words God's grace is manifest as the very fabric of creation, and the study of creation, the natural world and the laws that govern it, will reveal that grace to anyone with the intelligence to perceive it.

The world as Maimonides understood it is *tov,* just as Genesis had said: not in the sense of morally good, but necessarily perfect. That is to say, the world is exactly as it has to be if it is to survive. This understanding of goodness allows for lots of pain and suffering. Not every breast bears milk, and not every baby gets fed. There are earthquakes, accidents, murders, and diseases, but none of these diminishes the grace at creation's heart.

Maimonides's position is central to the thesis of this book: God's grace precludes nothing and guarantees nothing. It only provides for all possibilities, many of which will become actualities whether we like them or not. The world is *tov,* not in the sense of morally good, but physically sound. It is also *tohu va'vohu,* wild and unpredictable. The two are not in opposition. The world is *tohu va'vohu* because it is *tov,* and it is *tov* because it is *chesed.* The world is wild because it is creative, and it is creative because this is how it survives, and it survives because creativity is what God is and grace is what God does. And because creation is wild, Maimonides tells us that God's grace is wily.

Creation as a Window into God

Given the fact that God's "wily grace" (more on this phrase shortly) permeates the natural world, it only seems logical that understanding the natural world will bring us to at least a partial understanding of God. Again Maimonides: "Accordingly, whenever one of His actions is apprehended, the attribute from which this action proceeds is predicated of Him, may He be exalted, and the same deriving from that action is applied to Him."[5]

Creation acts as a window through which we can peer into and apprehend something of the nature of grace and hence the nature of God. When we do so, however, we must be careful not to anthropomorphize God, careful not to make God a larger version of ourselves.

For example, in Psalm 103 God is compared to a father who has compassion on his children (Psalm 103:13), and in the book of the prophet Malachi we are told that God will pity the faithful as parents spare their faithful children (Malachi 3:17). Maimonides warns us not to take such texts literally.

> It is not that He, may He be exalted, is affected and has compassion. But an action similar to that which proceeds from a father in respect to his child and that is attached to compassion, pity, and an absolute passion, proceeds from Him, may He be exalted, in reference to His holy ones, not because of a passion or a change. And just as

when we give a thing to somebody who had no claim upon us, this is called grace in our language—as it says: *Grant them graciously* [Judges 21:22] [so is the term applied to Him:] *Whom God hath graciously given* [Genesis 33:5]; because *God hath dealt graciously with me* [Genesis 33:11]. Such instances are frequent. For He, may He be exalted, brings into existence and governs beings that have no claim upon Him with respect to being brought into existence and being governed. For this reason He is called *gracious.*[6]

So creation's window is a dark one. We can get a sense of what God is by seeing what God does, but the doing of God is always greater than that small slice we can see. Remember God is a verb: not a Being but be- *ing* itself. So what we see in the world is an authentic slice of divine activity, but a slice only, and we must not mistake it for the whole of that activity.

Given this, however, the importance of Maimonides's teaching here is in his realization that people and creation have no claim on God. We didn't deserve to live any more than we deserve to die. We are simply an actualization of the infinite grace and possibility of God. God has no passion, meaning God didn't desire our existence or purposefully set out to create us, and God is unchanged by our existence, meaning that once we are created, God feels no special attachment to us.

Again, think of the relationship of sun to sunlight. The sun shines because it must, and it has no particular attachment to its rays. Indeed the sun doesn't perceive light as anything other than itself. From God's perspective, creation is just what it is to be God, and all that is created is simply a manifestation of God the way sunlight is a manifestation of the sun. It is we who imagine a distinction between creator, creativity, and creation. From God's perspective, these are and there is only God.

God's Wily Grace

Maimonides makes a point of speaking of God's "wily" grace. Something that is wily is something that is evasive, tricky, elusive, and even deceptive. Why associate God's grace with these attributes? Maimonides himself doesn't say, but I suggest the reason is this: grace is excess, and excess cannot be predicted or controlled. Grace operates in the wildly creative mode of *tohu va'vohu* outside human comprehension and acts in ways that we can neither predict nor avoid. *Chesed* is the trickster in that its creativity necessitates the morphing of one thing into another and eventually all things into their opposite. If you hope to cling to grace, you will find that the salvation you think you have grasped turns into the damnation you desperately sought to avoid.

God's grace is not a "Get Out of Jail Free" card or a "Go to Jail and Do Not Collect $200" card, but both at the same time. *Chesed* in itself isn't freeing, but understanding the nature of *chesed* is. *Chesed* is wily, tricky, unpredictable, and chaotic. It offers solace and desperation rather than the first in opposition to the second. Knowing *chesed* to be what it is, that is, the wily and wild excess of divine creativity doing what it does without purpose or goal, allows you to cultivate a radical acceptance of reality as it is in this very moment. And it is this radical acceptance that is at the heart of living graciously with the wily grace of God.

Grace, Excess, and A-reciprocity

Maimonides's wily grace is linked to divine excess. For him grace is the natural and unending effervescence of God that, from our point of view, manifests as the natural world of which we are a part. This means that God's grace flows of its own accord and not because the recipient of God's grace has some claim on God or deserves God's grace. In other words, there is no reason for God to create the world at all. God simply does it because it is God's nature to do it; the Creator must create but never for the sake of the creation, and always for the sake of—from the very nature of—the Creator itself.

Maimonides goes to great lengths to emphasize the free-flowing nature of divine grace and to free it and God from any notion of divine-human reciprocity. He even goes so far as to say there is no relation at all between God and creation.[7] What he means is that there is no reciprocal relationship between Creator and creation.

> A relation, then, is a bridge, an attribute that inheres in two substances at once and joins one to the other. If this is so, relation can only join things that resemble each other in some respect.... It follows that there is no possibility of a relation between a necessary being [God] and a contingent one [humanity, for example], for if there were, there would be an attribute that inheres in God and links the divine essence to something else. This would mean that God is affected by and in some sense dependent on a part of creation, and this, for Maimonides, just cannot be.[8]

If there is no reciprocity between God and creation, there is certainly no reciprocity between God and humanity, humanity being a part of creation. God is not affected by the existence of humans or anything we humans may do. God doesn't love us, or pity us, or care for us the way we humans understand loving, pitying, and caring. Rather God creates and sustains us, but does so purely from the necessity of God's own nature. Again, we are left with a choiceless God who acts solely from the nature of what it is to be God.

Creation, Grace, and Time

As passionate as Maimonides is about promoting a nonreciprocal non-relationship between Creator and creation, he is equally passionate about taking God out of time as well:

> I have already made it known to you that the foundation of the whole Law is the view that God has brought the world into being out of nothing without there having been a temporal beginning. For time is created, being consequent upon the motion of the sphere, which is created.[9]

According to Maimonides, God's creation happened without time. Time, he says, is dependent on the movement of the earth (the sphere) in relation to the sun, and the sun isn't created until the fourth day. Creation "happened," although without time it is impossible to say something happened. There is no "was" or "will be" without time, and God, being beyond time, operates in the timeless "now." The "beginning" expressed in Genesis 1:1 is a creation out of time, and a creation out of time is not once upon a time, but timeless. Thus God is creating the universe even now: "Now the world was not created in a temporal beginning, as we have explained, for time belongs to the created things."[10]

The reason this matters is that if God is outside time, and creation and time arise together, then any notion that God bestows grace upon us in response to who we are or what we do is false. God is not influenced by time or the doings of the time-bound. If grace is the very nature of existence, as Maimonides says, it is not dependent on that existence. That is to say, God's grace is the natural outpouring of God's infinite excess and is not aimed at or restricted by or to anything or anyone. Nor can grace be limited to any quality: life rather than death, blessing rather than curse, good rather than evil, and so on. God's grace is existence itself, life and death, blessing and curse, good and evil, everything and its opposite. Or, as Maimonides puts it: wily.

A Purposeless Driven Life

It is common to hear people claim that God created life for a purpose, that human life is thus purpose driven, and that the purpose that drives human life, or the purpose that ought to drive human life if humans understood the true nature of life, is to love God. Maimonides finds this idea ridiculous. Why, he asks, does God need to be loved?

> Even if the universe exists for the sake of man, and the final end of man is, as has been said, to worship God, a question remains to be asked regarding the final end of this worship. For He, may He be exalted, would not acquire greater perfection if He were worshipped by all that He has created and were truly apprehended by them, nor would He be attained by a deficiency if nothing whatever existed except Him.[11]

In other words, God gains nothing from creation, not even from the creation of human beings. God doesn't need us or our love and worship. And while it may be comforting to imagine that God does need us, the fact is otherwise: we exist for no purpose whatsoever. We exist simply because it is the nature of God's creative grace that existence happens, and in our tiny speck of the universe that creativity resulted in us.

Of course, not all Jewish thinkers think this way. Rabbi Abraham Joshua Heschel, for example, drawing on the notion that humanity does have a purpose and that purpose is to complete the work of creation by bringing the world into alignment with justice and compassion, would argue against the notion of grace presented in this book.

From Maimonides to Spinoza

We can deepen our understanding of grace and of creation as an expression of grace even further by moving from Moses Maimonides in the twelfth century to Baruch Spinoza in the seventeenth century. Where Maimonides was influenced by the writings of Alexander of Aphrodisias, Spinoza was influenced by Maimonides.

When asked about the purpose of creation, Spinoza echoes Maimonides: *Quia ei non defuit materia,* "It is the nature of God to give existence to all forms capable of existence."[12] Spinoza speaks of God as *deus sive natura,* "God or nature," and in so doing gives us a powerful understanding of God as a verb so central to our understanding of grace.

The *natura* in *deus sive natura* is not as straightforward as the English translation "nature" might have us believe. If by nature we mean the created world, the universe with its myriad planets and stars, the fullness of the physical world from quarks to quasars, then we reduce God to nature and can do away with the word "God" altogether. And if we do this, we have lost not only Spinoza's God but Maimonides's God as well.

There are two understandings of *natura* in Spinoza's work: *natura naturata* and *natura naturans,* and they couldn't be more different:

By *Natura naturans* we must understand what is in itself and is conceived through itself, *or* such attributes of substance as express an eternal and infinite essence, that is ... God, insofar as he is considered as a free cause. But by *Natura naturata* I understand whatever follows from the necessity of God's nature, *or* from God's attributes, that is, all the modes of God's attributes insofar as they are considered as things which are in God, and can neither be nor be conceived without God.[13]

In other words, *natura naturans* is "nature naturing," whereas *natura naturata* is the result of nature naturing. When Spinoza says *deus sive natura,* "God or nature," he is referring to *natura naturans,* or nature naturing. God is the creative process, and that aspect of the process open to human investigation is what we call nature. *Natura naturans* is God god- *ing; natura naturata* is the result of that god-*ing:* you, me, and the universe as a whole.

The created world is part of God, the way sunlight is a part of the sun. And, as with suns and sunlight, God is greater than the sum of God's creation. God is creativity itself, and not just the things that arise from it. God is creating not by choice or will, but by the very nature of what it is to be God. Neither Maimonides nor Spinoza reduces God to nature, and each posits a God that embraces nature while at the same time transcending nature. For both philosophers, God is a verb.

God Is What God Does

God is what God does, and what God does is create. God is not a being, but be- *ing* itself. God is not the Creator, but creativity. And the answer to why God does what God does is that it is God's nature to do so.

We have demonstrated ... that Nature does not act with an end in view; that the eternal and infinite being, whom we call God, or Nature *[natura naturata],* acts by the same necessity whereby it exists. That the necessity of his nature whereby he acts is the same as that whereby he exists has been demonstrated.... So the reason or cause why God, or nature, acts and the reason or cause why he exists, are one and the same. Therefore just as he does not exist for an end, so he does not act for an end; just as there is no beginning or end to his existing, so there is no beginning or end to his acting.[14]

This endless activity for its own sake is what we mean by grace.

I have now explained the nature and properties of God: that he necessarily exists, that he is one alone, that he is and acts solely from the necessity of his own nature, that he is the free cause of all things and how so, that all are in God and so dependent on him that they can neither be nor be conceived without him, and lastly, all have been predetermined by God, not from his free will or absolute pleasure, but from the absolute nature of God, his infinite power.[15]

God is unconditioned and hence God's actions are unconditioned, and because they are unconditioned, they are done without external cause. There is nothing you can do to get God to do anything. God is what God does, and what God does God does freely, unconditionally. Anything less would have God act as a puppet manipulated by those who know how to pull God's strings.

Neither Maimonides nor Spinoza believes in this kind of God. Their God cannot be enticed or repelled by human behavior. Where they differ is on the relationship between God and creation. For Maimonides, God is always other; for Spinoza, God is all and there is no other. Maimonides has to fashion a bridge between Creator and creation that allows for the former to fashion the latter. Spinoza is in no need of a bridge, for there is no separation between Creator and creation.

Spinoza erases the distinction between Creator and creation by shifting from nouns to verbs: God isn't a static "is" but an endless "is- *ing";* God isn't a doer but a doing. And what God does is create, and what God creates is the infinite possibility of being. And all of this is done for no reason whatsoever. Reality is because God is. And, again, this is what we mean by grace: *God's unlimited, unconditional, unconditioned, and all-inclusive love for all creation* expressed as the every existence of all creation.

To Beneficence and Beyond

Just as we are removing purpose from God, and therefore from God's creation, we must be careful to remove benefit from God and creation as well. God didn't create the world for our sake. God did what God did and does what God does because God could not and cannot do otherwise. Yet, as Maimonides told us when commenting on Psalm 89, "The meaning of *chesed* is excess in whatever matter excess is practiced. In most cases, however, it is applied to excess in beneficence."

In other words it is better to be than not to be. There is no question. And while being means confronting both life and death, blessing and curse, the joy of being somehow outweighs its sorrow, and with some very sad exceptions, most us prefer to live than to die. Hence the sense that God's grace is beneficent.

At least *in most cases;* most, but not all. The unlimited and unconditioned God overflows with excess, and this excess flows out into and as time and space and ultimately matter, but because it is limitless excess, it cannot be constrained by human categories of good and bad.

Creation happens because God is *Ehyeh asher Ehyeh,* the be- *ing* whose is- *ing* is all reality. Because *Ehyeh* is limitless creativity, some of what is created is beneficent and some is not. God isn't good or bad. Creation isn't good or bad. God is the happening of all reality in potential, and creation is the happening of all reality in actuality, and you and I are part of this happening. While we may judge the happening of God against our own desires and thus label some things "good" and others "bad," God is not constrained by our labels at all. Everything that can happen will happen, for the infinite creativity of God necessitates it.

Does Creation Have a Point?

Creation is an act of grace. There is no compulsion in it and no necessity for it. God didn't choose to create the world, but did so for no other reason than it is God's nature to do so. God's nature and nature herself are inextricably linked to one another and to *chesed.* But is there a point to any of it?

Rabbi Chaim Vital (1543–1620) tells us that God created the world because God "wished to reveal the complete array and perfection of His powers and deeds."[16] Writing a century later, Rabbi Schneur Zalman tries to get around Vital's notion of God, wishing to accomplish something by speaking of God's "desire" and insisting that regarding desire "one may ask no questions." What he means by this is that desires aren't rational; they simply arise in us as part and parcel of who we are, so there is no point in trying to determine why God desires what God desires.

In other words, God's desire to create simply arises in God because creating is God's nature. The created world and everything in it is desired by God the way we might say an apple tree desires to produce apples or an acorn desires to be an oak tree. In this way we might say that an infinite God desires infinite possibility, some of which become actualized reality. Taking this one step further, Rabbi Zalman cites and criticizes a Rabbinic teaching that God created the universe because God desired a dwelling place in the physical world *(Midrash Tanchuma, Naso* 7:1), claiming that the distinction between physical and spiritual worlds has no standing, since "God pervades all reality equally."[17]

So, if God is the very is- *ing* of creation, and God creates because creating is what it is to be God, does creation have a point or purpose? I suggest the answer to that question is no. If creation had a point or a purpose, then the act of creation would be conditioned by that point or purpose. And if creation is for the purpose of something other than creation,

creation is a means to an end and not an act of grace in and of itself.

There is no reason for the creation of the world. God creates because creating is the nature of God. When in our morning liturgy (prior to the blessing for light and creation) we read that God "renews creation daily," we are saying that creation never ceases because God never ceases.

> It is an axiom, a general principle, that [God] created the entire universe, and having done so, never withdraws from the universe for even a single moment.... We pay tribute to this in our daily prayers when we say, "He creates and fashions (present tense) light, and He creates darkness." When speaking of any accomplishments of [God]'s creatures, however, we speak of them in the past tense.... This means that [God] is part of every creature He ever created, and once man realized that he is nothing without [God] Who has created him and Who provides him with all the strength and creative stimuli that he possesses, he will be able to relate to Hashem as an ongoing creative Force in His universe.

> *(KEDUSHAT LEVI, B'REYSHIT* 1:1)[18]

The purposelessness of God is hard for many to grasp. How can it be that God lacks purpose? Isn't the purpose of God to create, guide, and judge creation? If there is no purpose to God, why is there a God in the first place?

To answer these questions, ask them this way: Which comes first, God or God's purpose? If you say God comes before purpose, then you are positing a God without purpose who at some point makes up a purpose. If you say purpose comes before God, you have to then explain who creates this purpose, and how is it that there is a time when purpose exists and God does not, and how is God created to fulfill this purpose?

It seems to me you have only three options here: (1) God exists without purpose, (2) purpose exists without God, or (3) God and God's purpose are one in the same. I opt for the last. God doesn't have a purpose; God is purposeful. The purpose of God is God's nature, and the nature of God is to manifest reality, and reality includes both life and death, blessing and curse, and so on. And since God does all this without external motive, it is all an act of supreme grace.

Purpose? No. Direction? Yes.

Saying that there is no point or purpose to creation, that creation is an act of grace unearned and undeserved (after all, prior to creation there was nothing in existence to earn or deserve anything), is not the same, however, as saying that there is no direction to creation.

The creation story in Genesis 1 is a tale of grace without point or purpose, but it is also a tale of grace with a definite direction. The process of creation leads from mineral, to vegetable, to animal, to human, that is, from less inclusive to more inclusive levels of consciousness. The direction of life, flowing effortlessly and without extraneous point or purpose, is toward more and more inclusive degrees of consciousness. The story ends with the creation of humanity, but that is only because we humans wrote it. There is no reason to believe that creation's direction ends with us or with the level of consciousness we have as yet attained. Creation may be the inexorable flow of God incarnating as the world, a flow that will eventually lead to a level of consciousness capable of realizing that all life, including itself, is the grace-filled flowing of God.

But if this is so, can't we then say that the purpose of creation is to become aware of itself as the incarnation of God? No, not if we are to preserve the notion of grace as unconditioned. If God creates in order to achieve some specific level of creation, then creation is contingent upon that level, and everything beneath that level is *lo tov,* not yet what it should be.

The fact that each act of creation is *tov,* sufficient unto itself, suggests that each new act is unconditioned and hence grace-filled. God is not looking for something or someone in particular. God simply creates. The fact that creation may give rise to beings capable of self-realization (aware of themselves as apart *from* God) is an interesting aspect of creation but not its point, and the possibility that these self-realized beings may some day become Self-realized (aware of themselves as a part *of* God) is all the more astonishing, but again not the purpose of creation itself. But it may be the direction of creation.

God can only be God, and to be God is to create worlds, and to create worlds is to set in motion the possibility of minds emerging over time and through natural selection that are capable of knowing God in, with, and as all creativity and creation. But such minds are not the point of creation, only the latest tip of the direction creation, at least as we perceive it, seems to take.

Chapter 3

Grace & Humanity

From Grace to Utility

What was true about creation as a whole as revealed in Genesis 1 is no less true about the creation of humankind: there is no point to it or reason for it. After creating and affirming the goodness of beasts and bugs (Genesis 1:25), God suddenly says, "Let us make humankind *[adam]* in our image, mirroring our likeness. They shall have dominion over the fish of the sea, and over the birds of the air, over the cattle, and over the wild animals of the earth *[eretz]"* (Genesis 1:26).

You might be inclined to say that the reason for humanity's creation is to rule the fish, the birds, the cows, and so forth, but this isn't what Torah says. The animals' survival isn't contingent on the creation of humanity. God isn't commanding the superiority of humankind; God is simply noting it. People will rule over the earth the way cattle eat grass: it is their nature to do so. But the earth doesn't need a ruler, and Genesis 1 doesn't give a reason for God's creation of humankind. This is very different from the creation story found in Genesis 2:

This is the history of sky and earth from the time they were created. When the God *YHVH* made earth and sky, there was no vegetation on the earth and no herbs had sprouted from the ground, for the God *YHVH* had not yet brought rain to the earth, and there was not yet anyone to till the soil....

(GENESIS 2:4–5)

In this story, the creation of man (woman coming a bit later) and rain is utilitarian: God seems to want vegetation to sprout and cannot achieve this without rain and gardeners. The point of creation in this chapter, unlike the previous one, is to produce vegetation, and the purpose of humanity is to facilitate that production. People are necessary to God's plan, and the creation of humanity is an act of necessity rather than grace. This is made all the more clear by what God creates after having created the human:

The God *YHVH* then planted a garden in Eden, in the east, and put the human he had formed there. And then the God *YHVH* caused the ground to grow every tree that was pleasing to the sight and good for food, with the Tree of Life in the middle of the garden along with the Tree of Knowledge of Good and Evil. A river sprung up from Eden to water the garden, and it divided into four branches.

(GENESIS 2:8–10)

The creation of *adam* was for the purpose of tending the garden. God made sure that what grew in the garden would please and sustain the human so that he would stay engaged with his work of cultivation. But the garden wasn't for the sake of the human, but rather the human for the garden.

The First Threat

The creation of *adam* in Genesis 1 is without purpose and hence an act of pure grace. The creation of *adam* in Genesis 2 is with purpose and hence an act of pure utility. And because there is a purpose to humanity—tending the garden—and because the garden, which seems to be the point of creation in Genesis 2, cannot survive without this tending, and, as we will learn as the story progresses, eating from the Tree of Knowledge will somehow interfere with humanity's purpose, God has got to do something that helps ensure the human will adhere to the purpose for which he was created. So after creating *adam* and the garden, God creates something very different: the first threat.

> The God *YHVH* took *adam* and placed him in the garden of Eden, to till it and tend it. And the God *YHVH* commanded *adam,* saying, "You are free to eat of every tree of the garden with the exception of the Tree of Knowledge of Good and Evil; of this tree you must not eat; and if you do, you will die instantly."

(GENESIS 2:15–17)

Genesis 1 knows nothing of this. This is because in that story humanity is an incarnation of divine grace without any purpose beyond itself. Genesis 1 knows nothing of gardens, a Tree of Knowledge, or the death threat that comes with it. Threats arise only when there is a need to coerce someone into doing something they may not want to do on their own. What is it God wants the human to do? Tend the rest of creation. Why might eating from the Tree of Knowledge derail this plan? Torah doesn't say. And if eating from the Tree of Knowledge would derail God's purpose for the human, why create the tree in the first place? Again Torah doesn't say. It might be that God couldn't do otherwise, but the purposeful nature of this creation story seems to put that in doubt.

You might imagine that the command not to eat from the Tree of Knowledge was simply a test of human obedience. But why is this necessary? Why does God, who created *adam* for the sole purpose of tending the garden, imagine that *adam* would or could do anything else? *Adam's* very existence is for the purpose of this tending; it is in his DNA, isn't it?

With regard to grace, Genesis 2 is as different from Genesis 1 as one can imagine. The grace-filled creation of humanity in the first story leaves humankind free. The utilitarian creation of *adam* in the second story leaves humanity bound by law. The only freedom *adam* has open to him is the freedom of rebellion. Listen to this carefully: *in a world of grace, play is the norm; in a world of law, rebellion is the norm.*

Grace and Play

This bears some investigation. In the book of Proverbs we find yet another creation story. In this version of creation, the first manifestation of God's creating is *Chochma,* Lady Wisdom:

> I was there from the beginning,
> from before there was a beginning.
> I was before depth was conceived,
> before springs bubbled with water,
> before the shaping of mountains and hills,
> before God fashioned the earth and its bounty
> before the first dust settled on the land.
> When God prepared the heavens, I was there...
> I stood beside God as firstborn and friend.
> My nature is joy, and I gave God constant delight.
>
> (PROVERBS 8:23–27, 8:30)[1]

As in Genesis 1, there is no reason for the creation of Wisdom; she simply emerges from God. Wisdom is an expression of God's grace, and according to Proverbs, her nature is pure joy. Wisdom dances before God as a source of endless delight, and with the creation of the incarnate world, she rejoices in it as well as delighting in humankind (Proverbs 8:31). Wisdom plays like a young child (Proverbs 8:30); she plays for the sheer joy of playing. There is no need to coerce Wisdom into delighting God and taking delight in humankind; it is simply her nature to do so. Hence there is no commanding of one thing or prohibiting of another in this version of creation. Everything flows graciously from God and acts according to its nature, as does God.

The promise offered in this section of the book of Proverbs is that we can listen to Wisdom and follow her. This means that we too can live graciously; we too can make of life play. This is what a grace-filled existence is: pure play. Yet even in play there are winners and losers, successes and failures, so please don't imagine that a playful life is a life of blessing without curse. There is no such life.

The difference between living with grace and living without grace is this: a grace-filled person, a person who accepts the wily grace of God as it comes, both the good and the bad, the joys and the horrors, accepts both as part of the play, while the grace-less person, a person who is offered no less grace than the other but who refuses to accept that grace, imagining that one can live without suffering and that suffering is a sign of disfavor, lives fearfully lest such disfavor be incurred.

While you may prefer to win rather than to lose, to rejoice rather than to grieve, don't imagine the hardships and losses of life are punishments or signs of divine disfavor. You know that to live is to receive the grace of God, the fullness of life—birth and death, blessing and curse—and that to live well and wisely—to play in life rather than to earn a living—means, to paraphrase Deuteronomy 6:5, engaging each moment with all your heart, all your soul, and all your might.

Genesis 1 and Proverbs 8 share the grace-filled aspect of creation. Genesis 2 and 3 are almost the antithesis of it.

Grace and Rebellion

In a world of grace we do what we wish, because what we wish is to be of benefit to others. Being creatures of grace, we become bestowers of grace. In a world of utility where our value is determined not by our existence but by our service, we do what we are commanded to do, while what we wish to do is rebel. The rebellion in Genesis 3 isn't arbitrary, however. It isn't rebellion for rebellion's sake. The issue of rebellion and disobedience is linked to wisdom.

> When the woman saw that the tree was good for eating and a delight to the eyes, and that the tree was desirable as a source of wisdom, she took of its fruit and ate.
>
> (GENESIS 3:6, JPS)

The woman (later to be named *Chava*/Eve, the Mother of the Living [Genesis 3:20]) realizes that the fruit of the Tree of Knowledge would most likely taste delicious, but this is not enough to motivate her to violate God's prohibition against eating it. Nor is the added realization of the fruit's beauty sufficient incentive to do so. Only when she realizes that by eating the fruit of the Tree of Knowledge she will become wise does she pluck the fruit and eat it. Wisdom is the motivator of her rebellion.

In Proverbs, Wisdom seeks out humanity and delights in us. She prepares a fine meal for us (Proverbs 9:2) and sends her servant girls to call us to her banquet (Proverbs 9:3). She gives of herself freely, telling us that those who find her find life, and those who refuse the gift of her presence court death. The meaning of this is simple enough: live wisely and you live graciously, and your life is playful and fearless; live unwisely and you live ungraciously, fearing God and seeking to earn what is actually freely given. And because you imagine you must earn a living rather than playfully live your life, you live in a perpetual state of exhaustion, worried that you can never do enough to please God.

In Genesis 2, wisdom is very different. God in this story wants to keep wisdom from humankind. Why? Perhaps because wisdom leads to play, and God created humans for work. Whatever the reason, the consequence of eating from the Tree of Knowledge is very different from that of dining with Wisdom herself.

So the as-yet-to-be-named Eve rebels against the utilitarian nature of her existence and reaches for wisdom to free herself from it. The parallel between the rebellious woman reaching for that which Lady Wisdom freely offers should not be lost on us. Perhaps the author of Genesis 3 has the story of Lady Wisdom in mind. Perhaps the author is saying, if you cannot imagine Lady Wisdom giving us wisdom, then imagine a lady stealing it for us. In either case wisdom comes to humanity through the feminine. Things are very different with her man.

> And she also gave some to her man who was
> with her, and he ate.

(GENESIS 3:6)

Adam (in this story no longer representing all humanity, male and female, but the specific male from which the female was created) eats without any intentionality at all. The woman offers him the forbidden fruit and he eats it. Torah doesn't tell us why, and this lack of information coming as it does immediately after the woman's deliberative act of rebellion for the sake of wisdom suggests that wisdom is anything but a motivator for the man. He eats because it is offered to him. He eats mindlessly, and by so doing he achieves not joy and play but fear and shame (Genesis 3:10).

In the Proverbs story, Wisdom is the blueprint of creation and a force for actively shaping the world and delighting in its human inhabitants. In the Proverbs story, we learn that humanity is created to be happy and that the way to happiness is to become wise (Proverbs 8:32). In Genesis 2 and 3, there is no talk of happiness, and wisdom, when mentioned, is prohibited.

Historically these are two different stories written by two different authors, but, again, I cannot help but link one to the other by noting the role of wisdom in the woman's rebellion. It is Eve's desire for wisdom, prohibited in Genesis and yet freely given in Proverbs, that links her to Lady Wisdom. The message is this: in a grace-filled world, wisdom is abundant and free; in a world lacking grace, wisdom is rare and prohibited. In a grace-filled world, there is no fear or coercion; in a world lacking grace, these are its defining characteristic.

Which world do you inhabit? Let me suggest that the answer depends not on which story of creation is true, but on which story of creation shapes your own thinking. If you see the world as grace-filled, you will seek wisdom for yourself and others. If you see the world as grace-less, you will, if you are like Adam, think nothing of wisdom, or if you are like Eve, you will rebel and grasp it regardless of the risks. While demonized for millennia, Eve is the true hero of the Genesis story, a Hebrew Prometheus stealing wisdom from God and, albeit prematurely, sharing it with her man.

A Rabbinic Perspective

Where I see rebellion for the sake of wisdom a praiseworthy act, the early Rabbis saw humanity's rebellious side as problematic. Knowing, as God must, that humanity would be rebellious, why would God create humanity in the first place?

> Rabbi Berekiah taught: When the Holy Blessed One contemplated creating humanity, God thought, "If I create humanity, both the wicked and the just will spring from them; to avoid the former must I preclude the latter, and not create humankind at all?"
>
> How did the Holy One decide? God ignored the potential for wickedness and aligned solely with grace. And thereby humans were created.
>
> *(GENESIS RABBAH 8:4)*

In other words, according to Rabbi Berekiah, God didn't see rebellion as a deal breaker in the creation of humankind. God was willing to ignore it and trust the power of grace to deal with any rebellions that might arise. Rabbi Berekiah's colleague Rabbi Simon had a different view:

> When the Holy Blessed One was about to create humankind, the angels divided into arguing camps, some urging the creation of humans,

some opposing it. The Angel of Love said, "Create them, for they will know love." The Angel of Truth said, "Don't create them, for they will know lies." What did God do? God grabbed the Angel of Truth and cast it to the earth.

(GENESIS RABBAH 8:5)

Here too God was aware of the dark side of human nature and yet chose to create us anyway. Why? Again no reason is given. There is something in the nature of God that leads to the creation of humanity. It isn't a matter of humans being worthy of life, but of God being undeterred by our creation. The Psalmist, too, seems to see things this way:

When I contemplate the vastness of heaven,
the work of Your fingers,
the moon and the stars set in their places;
what are humans that You are mindful of them?
Temporary persons that You care for them?
And yet You made them just a little less than
 divine,
and crowned them with glory and dignity.
You have placed them in charge of Your
 creation,
and set the world at their feet:
sheep, oxen, all the beasts of the earth, birds
 of the sky,
and

fish of the sea, and whatever traverses the
ocean's currents.

(PSALM 8:4–9)

The question is asked—why are humans elevated above the rest of creation?—but no answer is given. At best the psalm ends with a non sequitur: rather than answer his own question, the Psalmist simply proclaims, "O *YHVH* our Sovereign, how majestic is Your name in all the earth!" (Psalm 8:10).

This isn't an answer at all, but an affirmation that no answer is possible. Why are humans as they are? Because God is as God is. God being God necessitates creation in general and, in the case of our tiny speck of the universe, the creation of humans as well. Grace, God's wily excess, God's infinite effervescence, is the reason for all creation, human and otherwise. God's grace necessitates creation. And perhaps it is the wiliness of God that cannot help but manifest as us wily humans who cannot help but surprise ourselves with the excesses of our own personalities. Being created in the image of God may mean that we too are creatures of excess and exuberance, creatives whose actions are as wily as any done by our Creator.

God is limited to being God, and being God means creating, and in time creating beings like you and me. God is reality, the primordial creativity that gives rise to everything from quarks to quasars, and the dark energy and dark matter that surround and permeate them. There is nothing that isn't a part of God, for to say, "This isn't God," is to place a limitation on God that makes God finite, and a finite god isn't God.

If God is infinite, if God is all that was, is, and will ever be, in what sense can God need anything, since there isn't anything other than God that could be needed? God "needs" and "desires" only one thing, and that is to be God. God is limited only by the necessity of being God. God cannot be other than what God is, and what God is necessitates creation in all its complexity and wiliness.

Given that this is a book about grace, our focus is naturally on those stories that reveal grace. When it comes to the creation of humankind, it is Genesis 1 that offers us the deepest insight into the connection between humanity and grace.

> Then God said, "Let us make humankind *[adam]* in our image, mirroring our likeness. They shall have dominion over the fish of the sea, and over the birds of the air, over the cattle, and over the wild animals of the earth *[eretz],* and over every creeping thing that creeps upon earth." So God created humankind in the divine image, in the image of God they were created; male and female God created them.

> (GENESIS 1:26–27)

To understand the nature of grace and its connection to humanity in this text, we will focus on four key words: *adam* (humanity), *tzelem* (image), *demut* (likeness), and *yarad* (dominion).

Adam, the Alter Ego of God

Adam is not yet a proper name in this text, but a noun best translated as "humanity" or "earthling." Translating *adam* this way draws out the Hebrew pun linking *adam* (earthling) to *adamah* (earth) that is made explicit in Genesis 2:7, "Then the God *YHVH* formed an earthling from the dust of the earth and breathed life into him through his nostrils, and the earthling came alive." Since in this version of creation *adam* is made of *adamah,* the pun is clear, and the translation of *adam* as "earthling" makes perfect sense and is far superior to the more traditional rendering, "man." The problem with Genesis 1 is that the text doesn't refer to the earth as *adamah* but as *eretz,* "land," and hence the pun, if pun is intended, fails miserably.

So let's assume that no pun is intended and the author of Genesis 1 isn't linking *adam* to *adamah* at all. This is precisely the argument made by Rabbi Samson Raphael Hirsch, one of the great Jewish sages of the nineteenth century. He argues that the wordplay in Genesis 1 isn't between *adam* and *adamah,* earthling and earth, but between *adam* and *adom,* the human being and the color red, the least broken ray of the light spectrum. God, being the full spectrum of light, creates a ray that approximates wholeness while not yet being whole. Humanity, as Rabbi Hirsch puts it, is "the alter ego of the Supreme Being."[2]

The idea of alter ego, from the Latin meaning "the other I," was coined in the early nineteenth century by psychologists seeking to describe dissociative identity disorder.[3] Rabbi Hirsch, writing in the same century, clearly found this new term engaging, but I doubt he saw God as suffering from some malady. I suspect, instead, that Hirsch saw the human being as an extension of the Divine, just as a wave of the ocean is an extension of the ocean.

Imagine for a moment that both ocean and wave are conscious and that the ocean is aware of every wave as an extension of itself. There is, from the ocean's perspective, nothing but ocean. Now apply this metaphor to God and creation: there is, from God's perspective, nothing but God. The wave, on the other hand, mirroring the oceanic perspective from its own limited line of sight, sees itself as unique and perhaps even apart from (rather than a part of) the ocean on which it imagines itself sitting. Looking around at other waves, it doesn't see a unity or even an interconnectedness, but a series of separate albeit temporary "lives" birthing and dying all around it.

Following this analogy, we can say that from God's vantage point, creation is a single expression of divine effervescence: God's grace. From the human's vantage point, creation is a series of diverse entities, each with its own unique identity and destiny.

Now let's expand the analogy to take into account the notion that God isn't limited to distinctions such as ocean and wave. Let's say God is wetness itself, that essence that is the same whether we are speaking of ocean or wave. From the perspective of wetness (and I know this playful analogy is difficult for some to grasp, but I do ask that you try), there is no ocean or wave, only wetness. In this analogy, the true non-duality of God embraces and transcends the duality of ocean and wave in the greater wholeness of wetness.

God being a verb, *YHVH* or *Ehyeh,* the free-flowing unconditional activity of be- *ing,* God manifests as both ocean and wave, for this is what God's nature requires; God must be everything—the whole and all its parts. In this way God comes to know itself as part (the wave) and as whole (the ocean) while being something greater still (wetness).

Creation is to God what the ocean is to wetness. Humans are to God what waves are to wetness. God is both, and each is connected to and yet distinguishable from the other as well. It is the nature of God to create the whole and the part.

This said, we must be careful not to imagine, as Rabbi Vital did, that God creates the world *in order* to perceive reality from the perspective of seemingly separate beings. This implies that God could choose not to perceive the world from this perspective and hence could choose not to create the universe in general and humanity in particular. But this would be like saying the ocean could choose not to wave. The infinity of God necessitates the finite. God must include all things, for as long as something is other than God, outside of God, then God is boundaried, and a boundaried god isn't God.

The Silent God-Bearer

Rabbi Hirsch thinks much the same way in his discussion of the word *tzelem* (image). *Tzelem,* as Hirsch puts it, refers to the physical form or "sheath"[4] that carries the light of God into the world. Humanity is the God-bearer, though not bearing the entirety of God. In addition to being the sheath of godliness, humanity is also *damah,* a word most English translators read as "likeness" but which Hirsch links to *d'mamah,* "silence." This word is most well-known from the prophet Elijah's experience of God told in 1 Kings:

[YHVH] said, "Go out and stand on the mountain before *YHVH,* and *YHVH* will pass by." Now a terrible wind picked up, splitting mountains and shattering rocks before *YHVH,* but *YHVH* was not in the wind; then the wind died down and a violent quaking overtook the earth, but *YHVH* was not in the quaking; then the earthquake stilled and a blazing fire erupted, but *YHVH* was not in the fire; then the fire ceased, replaced by a sound of sheer silence *[d'mamah dakah].* When Elijah heard it, he wrapped his face in his cloak and went out and stood at the entrance of the cave.

Then a voice came upon him saying, "What are you doing here, Elijah?"

(1 KINGS 19:11–13)

According to Rabbi Hirsch, humanity represents God on earth; we are God's alter ego. Our bodies sheath or incarnate the light of God, and at our core is a silence that allows us to realize our godliness. When we tap that silence, our egoic will is silenced, and we can do nothing to "contradict the divine truth, love, justice, and holiness."[5] It is in this state of silence that we hear the Silence of God and realize what we are: God manifest as human the way ocean manifests as wave.

God is not in the wind: our doing and shattering and shaping; the wind is in/with God. God is not in our quaking: our fear, awe, and wonder; the quaking is in/with God. God is not in the fire: our passions, desires, and will; the fire is in/with God. God is not in the sheer silence; the sheer silence is in/with God, and when we enter that silence we realize that are in/with God as well. Pay special attention to the word *dakah*, "sheer." Something that is sheer is thin, so thin in this case as to be almost imperceptible—almost, for Elijah hears it. And so can we.

When we become silent, when we are not distracted by the blowing, quaking, and burning of the world, when we can stand still and accept what is as an expression of God's wily grace, we step into this sheer silence and hear the question at its core: what are you doing here? What are you doing with what you receive?

What Are You Doing Here?

The answer to God's question, the question that arises from the silence, is found in the book of the prophet Micah:

You know, Human, what is good and what *YHVH* requires of you: do justly, love *chesed,* and walk humbly with your God.

(MICAH 6:8)

You can only do justly when you love *chesed* and embrace reality as it is at each moment. And to do this you must humble yourself, silencing the egoic will and all its blowing, quaking, and burning in order to hear the challenge presented to you at each moment: what are you doing here? How are you using this moment—including moments of blowing, quaking, and burning—to promote justice and grace? We have said that there is no purpose to humanity's creation, but there is a task: to do justly, act gracefully, and humble the ego's selfishness that godliness might shine more brightly in the world.

Bringing Down the Light

This task revealed in the sheer silence of our inner encounter with our True Nature is what is meant by the term "dominion." We are here to have "dominion" over all living things. According to Rabbi Hirsch, the "fundamental meaning" of the Hebrew *radu* (dominion) is to "bring down from its free height into the hand, i.e., into your power."[6] And what we are to bring down is the light of God and the way of justice and *chesed* that comes when the world is so enlightened. In other words, to be fully human is to be God's alter ego, to be a bearer of divine light in the world, and to allow it to shine through the lives of the finite:

> If Man approaches the world as *adam,* the image and likeness of God, and demands its service only in service to God, then the earth gladly renders it, gladly recognizes Man as its ruler, his mastery is no enslavement or degradation, but rather a raising and elevation of all earthly material elements into the sphere of free-willed moral God-serving purposes. The whole world bows willingly to pure God-serving Man. But if Man misuses his position, if he does not approach the world as *adam,* as the representative of God, but in his own power of mastery, then animals too, do not willingly bow their necks to him.[7]

If we engage the world as *adam,* not as earth made conscious (as the pun *adam/adamah* would suggest), but as God made human (as the pun *adam/adom* would suggest), then when we engage with creation we do so not to bend creation to our will, but to align creation with the justice and compassion of Micah and the wisdom, joy, and delight of Proverbs. But engaging the world this way isn't a given. We can do otherwise, and when we do otherwise, the universe resists us at every turn.

Living the Likeness of God

Immediately following God's sharing the intent to create *adam* in the image and likeness of the Divine (Genesis 1:26), we read, "So God created humankind in the divine image, in the image of God they were created; male and female God created them" (Genesis 1:27). Notice that we are expecting creation in the image and likeness of God, but in the text itself we find only a reference to image. What happened to "likeness"?

To discover the meaning of this missing "likeness" think in terms of potential and actual. Adam is created as the image of God, that is, with the potential to sheath the divine and become God's alter ego, a God-bearer. But the realization of this potential is something that each of us must actualize for ourselves. This is the meaning of "likeness." We are born with the former; we must choose to manifest the latter. And choosing to live the likeness of God is what it means to engage the world as *adam,* the God-bearer.

Where is grace in this? First let us recall that grace is *God's unlimited, unconditional, unconditioned, and all-inclusive love for all creation.* Second, creation itself is an expression of grace, God's infinite effervescent excess; God's infinity necessitates the creation of the finite, for without the finite the infinite isn't in fact infinite. Third, it is the challenge of humanity to realize our true nature as light-bearers, God-bearers, God's alter ego, and only when we do realize this can we engage the world as *adam,* creating a world that reflects the light of God as and through justice and compassion. Grace in this context would require that God freely bestow on all humans this capacity for *adam* realization. And so God does. Recall Rabbi Simon's midrash about the arguing angels:

> When the Holy Blessed One was about to create humankind, the angels divided into arguing camps, some urging the creation of humans, some opposing it. The Angel of Love said, "Create them, for they will know love." The Angel of Truth said, "Don't create them, for they will know lies." What did God do? God grabbed the Angel of Truth and cast it to the earth."

(GENESIS RABBAH 8:5)

One way to understand this teaching is to say that God rejected Truth and created humankind out of love alone. This is a legitimate reading of the story, but not the only one. The eighteenth-century sage Rabbi Levi Yitzchak of Berditchev taught that God cast Truth to earth not as an act of punishment for having argued with God, but as a way of seeding creation with Truth so that those of us who engage creation correctly will discover the Truth about our own origin and nature.[8]

Let me summarize this chapter in this way: you and I, all human beings, are an expression of God manifest in and as the physical universe. We are God-bearers, the sheaths of divine light. We didn't deserve this gift of incarnation; we didn't earn it in some preexistent spirit world. We simply are it.

Our very existence is an act of divine grace. But the realization of our existence, the realization that we are God-bearers, and the actualization of that potential in the physical world aren't a given. Only the potential for realization is a given; the rest is up to us.

To realize this truth each of us must, like Elijah, hear the voice of sheer silence. Each of us must be addressed by the question, *What are you doing here?* What are you doing to help others realize their true nature as sheaths of God's light and thus live with wisdom, joy, and delight in the grace-filled exuberance that is God and God's world?

Chapter 4

Grace & Covenant

The central idea at the core of Judaism's self-understanding is *brit,* the covenant between God and the Jewish people. A covenant is a contract, and as with any contract each party to the contract agrees to uphold certain responsibilities vis-à-vis the other parties to the contract. There are two covenants mentioned in the Hebrew Bible. The first is between God and humanity as a whole; the second is between God and the Jewish people in particular.

The First Covenant

> God said to Noah and his sons, "I'm now establishing My covenant with you and your descendants, and with every living thing—birds, cattle, and every wild beast as well—all that have come out of the ark with you, every living thing on earth. I will maintain My covenant with you: never again shall floods destroy all life, never again shall there be a flood to destroy the earth."
>
> (GENESIS 9:8–11)

This covenant takes place after the Flood when the ark has landed and Noah sets about to repopulate the earth. In the passage just cited, we read God's side of the bargain: God will never again destroy the world with a flood. The conditions that humanity must uphold in order to merit God's side of the bargain are these:

> You may eat every living creature as well as all the green grasses. I give you all these. But don't eat flesh still saturated with its life-blood. The spilling of human blood, however, is forbidden, and requires a reckoning. Anyone, human or beast, who takes a human life must be brought to a reckoning, for humanity is made in God's image. Humans who shed human blood, their blood shall be shed. Be fertile, then, and increase; abound on the earth and thrive on it.
>
> (GENESIS 9:3–7)

If this seems awfully easy, you might take comfort in knowing that the ancient Rabbis felt the same. In fact they saw it as too easy, so, notwithstanding Torah's silence on the matter, they added to the covenant and invented the notion that God gave seven laws to Noah and his children rather than just the single law against homicide cited in Torah. These laws, called the Noahide Laws or the Seven Laws of Noah, are as follows:

> The children of Noah were commanded with seven commandments: [to establish] laws, and [to prohibit] cursing God, idolatry, illicit sexuality,

murder, robbery, and eating flesh from a living animal.

(TALMUD, *SANHEDRIN* 56a; cf. *TOSEFTA AVODAH ZARAH* 8:4, *(GENESIS RABBAH* 34:8)

According to Jewish tradition, anyone, Jew or Gentile, who adheres to the Laws of Noah is called righteous, and "the righteous people of all nations have a share in the World to Come" (Talmud, *Sanhedrin* 105a).

The Rainbow of All-Encompassing Grace

The sign of this covenant is the rainbow: "I have set My rainbow in the clouds as a sign of the covenant between Me and the earth" (Genesis 9:13). According to Rabbi Samson Raphael Hirsch, there are four reasons why God chose a rainbow as a sign of this covenant. First, a rainbow when compared to a hunting bow is a "reverse weapon," with its "strings" pointing toward the earth and its "arrow" pointing toward the sky, thus promising that God will never again sling arrows upon humankind. Second, a rainbow is an arc uniting heaven and earth and symbolizing harmony between them. Third, a rainbow is composed of light and water, suggesting that even in the midst of storms God's "preserving grace is still there."[1]

His fourth reason for the rainbow has to do with the rainbow's colors. The different colors would, Rabbi Hirsch taught, remind us that people develop in different ways, and only by honoring these differences can humanity as a whole progress toward the wisdom of knowing that we are created by grace as vehicles for grace.

> [The] future education to its godly purpose was to be founded just on these differences and varieties of humanity. For is the rainbow anything else but the one pure complete ray of light, broken up into seven degrees of seven colours, from the red rays nearest to the light to the violet, most distant from the light, losing itself into the darkness; and from the one to the other are they not all rays of light, and combined all together, do they not form one complete pure white ray?
>
> Could not this perhaps be meant to say: the whole manifold variety of all living creatures from the "most alive" Adam, the "red one," "Man," nearest to the godly, down to the lowest, humblest form of life in the humblest worm, ... God unites them all together in one common bond of peace, all fragments of one life, all refracted rays of the light?[2]

In other words, all beings are aspects of God's light, though some beings, *adam*/humanity in particular, are more capable than others of realizing the unity of light from Light. If Rabbi Hirsch is correct, and I am moved to accept his understanding of the rainbow, God's grace upon all life would translate into *adam*/humanity living that grace in relation to all life. And because, assuming humanity upheld its part of the covenant, humanity would live justly and compassionately and build a world on these virtues as well, there would never again be a need to destroy either the earth or the earthlings who live upon her.

It's a wonderful covenant, but there is a problem. Contractual obligations do not qualify as grace. Grace must be free and unconditional. If God's grace is offered only in exchange for righteousness, then it really isn't grace at all. So, in what sense can we understand the covenant as an act of grace?

The answer is found when Torah gives us a glimpse into the mind of God:

> And *YHVH* thought, "Never again will I doom the earth because of humanity, since from its youth the human mind schemes selfish schemes; nor will I ever again destroy every living being, as I have done. So long as the earth endures, seedtime and harvest, cold and heat, summer and winter, day and night shall not cease."

> (GENESIS 8:21–22)

God realizes that humans are by nature selfish. Since God is responsible for that nature, and hence for the wickedness humans are inclined to do, God realizes as well that punishing the earth over the deeds of earthlings is wrong. But this is not yet an act of grace, but of simple justice. God, not the earth, is responsible for the insanity of which people are capable.

Grace comes in when, knowing full well that the inclinations of humans can be wicked from their youth and that it is almost inevitable that humans will fail to live up to any bargain, God still chooses to make a covenant with them.

God is not acting rationally here. A rational decision would be along these lines: "Knowing that people are fundamentally incapable of keeping any promise if doing so no longer serves their self-interest, I will make no agreements with them but will simply lay out the consequences of violating My commandments."

This one-sided fiat would make more sense, but this isn't what God does. Instead, God makes a covenant with Noah and through Noah with all humankind. God's grace trumps God's reason. Humans don't merit a covenant with God, but God, being God, cannot help but offer them one.

As one who doesn't take Torah as history, for me the value of this story goes beyond any claim one might make for or against its historicity. What it says to me, whether or not it is history, is that God being God is grace unconditioned and unconditional. God enacts a covenant knowing full well the human partner will break it, because grace mandates that God do so, and God's grace triumphs over any other quality God may possess.

The Second Covenant

Where the first covenant, that between God and humanity, is grace-filled, with God promising not to destroy the world even though God knows that humans are incapable of living up to even the limited requirements placed upon them, the second covenant, that between God and the Israelites, is a more legalistic contract filled with rewards and punishments. Here is the reward:

If you walk according to My laws, keeping and conforming to My commandments, then I will give you rain in the rainy season, the land shall yield her bounty, and the fruit trees of the field shall bear much fruit.

(LEVITICUS 26:3–4)

This is how it shall be: if you scrupulously follow My commandments that I command you today—to love and serve *YHVH* your God with a whole heart and with every breath—then I will cause rain in the rainy season to fall on your land, the early rain and the later rain, that you may gather in your grain, your grapes, and your oil. And I will raise up pasture grass for your livestock, that you may eat and be filled.

(DEUTERONOMY 11:13–15)

And all these blessings will come upon you and embrace you, because you adhere to the voice of *YHVH* your God.... Blessed shall be the fruit of your body, the harvest of your ground, and the offspring of your herds.... *YHVH* will open the sky to you and give to your land its seasonal rains, and thereby bless all the labor of your hand. You shall lend to many nations, but you shall borrow from none.

(DEUTERONOMY 28:2, 28:4, 28:12)

And here is the punishment:

But if you are seduced to serve other gods and bow down to them, *YHVH's* anger will rise against you. *YHVH* will shut tight the sky so that no rain will fall and the earth will yield no produce, and you will quickly disappear from the good land that *YHVH* is giving you.

(DEUTERONOMY 11:16–17)

This is clearly a covenant, a contract, but is it evidence of God's grace? On the face of it, the answer must be no. Grace is unconditional, and this is a bargain: Do what I say, commands God, and I will bless you and your land. Don't do what I say and I will see you perish from the face of the earth. It is only if we define God's grace as reward for meritorious action and not as God's unconditional and unconditioned love that we can speak of *brit* as grace. Perhaps this is how the Psalmist understood grace in Psalm 136:

> Give thanks to YHVH...
> who slaughtered the firstborn of Egypt,
> for God's grace is unending;
> and liberated Israel out from among them,
> for God's grace is unending;
> with a powerful hand and an extended arm,
> for God's grace is unending;
> who severed the Sea of Reeds,
> for God's grace is unending;
> and caused Israel to pass through its midst,
> for God's grace is unending;
> who drowned Pharaoh and his army in the Sea of
> Reeds,
> for God's grace is unending;
> who guided his people through the wilderness,
> for God's grace is unending;
> who slew great kings,
> for God's grace is unending;
> and killed renowned rulers,
> for God's grace is unending;
> Sihon, king of the Amorites,
> for God's grace is unending;
> and Og, king of Bashan,
> for God's grace is unending;
> and gave their land to us as an inheritance,
> for God's grace is unending;

an inheritance to his servant Israel,
for God's grace is unending.
He remembered us in our shame,
for God's grace is unending;
and freed us from our enemies,
for God's grace is unending;
who gives food to all creatures,
for God's grace is unending.
O give thanks to the God of heaven,
for God's grace is unending.

(PSALM 136:1, 136:10–26)

Clearly, in the mind of the Psalmist, God's grace and Israel's history go hand in hand: the Exodus from Egypt is mentioned in verse 11, and the giving of the Promised Land is referenced in verses 21 and 22, and both are said to be expressions of God's enduring grace.

The Egyptians whose children were slaughtered in the Exodus (verse 10), of course, might find the verse assigned to them painfully offensive, and the parents, wives, and children of the Egyptian soldiers drowned in the Reed Sea no less so (verse 15), and one can imagine that the prior inhabitants of the Promised Land found God's grace anything but welcome, but for the Psalmist all these people are collateral damage in a campaign for the greater good—the good of Israel.

I mention the shadow side of God's grace not simply to throw a wet blanket on the Psalmist's enthusiasm for the destruction of Israel's enemies and his use of *chesed,* God's grace, to justify it, but so as not to lose sight of the fact that grace has an underbelly. What is beneficial to one may be tragedy to another, and yet still a matter of grace. It cannot be otherwise, for grace is not merited or earned; and because it isn't merited or earned, grace cannot be judged by any set of moral standards.

Is God Good?

The Psalmist's use of grace to justify actions that from the point of view of the non-Israelite are anything but gracious raises a crucial question: is God good? Before we can answer this question, we must pose another: what does it mean to be good? There is no definitive answer to this question, but for argument's sake let's take as our guide the Golden Rule as articulated by Rabbi Hillel: "What is hateful to you do not do to another" (Talmud, *Shabbat* 31a).

Given this answer to our second question—what is good?—we can now answer our first question: is God good? When God slaughters the firstborn of Egypt (Exodus 11:1–12:36), is this good? When God drowns the Egyptian soldiers (Exodus 14:27–28), is this good? When God decrees genocide on the inhabitants of the Promised Land—the Hittites, Amorites, Canaanites, Perizzites, Hivites, and Jebusites (Deuteronomy 20:17)—is this good?

Taking Hillel's Golden Rule as our definition of goodness, the answer to these questions is no. While benefiting the Israelites, God's actions were clearly not good for the Egyptians, Hittites, Amorites, Canaanites, Perizzites, Hivites, and Jebusites. Thus they fail the standard set by Hillel. Hillel's Golden Rule is universal and not limited to Jews. If we hold God to Hillel's standard, we have to argue that God is not good. If we argue otherwise, we are simply asserting that God is partisan.

Torah frequently treats God in this fashion, asserting that God is merely an agent controlling history in such a way that it comes out in the Jews' favor. God could have liberated the Hebrews enslaved in Egypt without tormenting the entire population of Egypt with plagues. God could have liberated them without the murder of the firstborn of Egypt. Similarly, when God split the Reed Sea and allowed the Israelites to pass through on dry land, God could have closed the sea before Pharaoh's soldiers were in its midst, thus saving the Israelites without causing a single unnecessary Egyptian death. Even regarding the Promised Land, God could have kept it free of inhabitants or could have caused the inhabitants to welcome the Israelites and convert to their faith, but God did none of this. Instead God commanded the Israelites to commit genocide:

> But of the cities of these people, which *YHVH* your God gives you as an inheritance, you shall let nothing live, you shall destroy them complete-

ly—the Hittites, and the Amorites, and the Canaanites, and the Perizzites, the Hivites, and the Jebusites—as *YHVH* your God commands you. You shall do this lest they teach you their wicked faith and in that way cause you to sin against *YHVH* your God.

(DEUTERONOMY 20:16–18)

Where is God's unconditional and unconditioned love in this mass slaughter of innocents? Did the God of Abraham, the God willing to submit to Abraham's definition of justice, morph into some other deity willing and eager to cause and sanction mass murder? Can it be that God's grace is conditional, and it is conditioned upon one being an Israelite? This would make sense if we assume that the God of Israel is only that: the God of Israel, and not the God of the whole world. But Genesis 1 and 2 make it clear that this is not the case.

God is the creator of earth and sky, this world and all worlds; God is the creator of humankind, all of whom are fashioned in God's image. So how is it that God prefers one people to all others? How is it that God frees the Hebrew slaves but not all slaves? Why is it that God uproots one people in order to settle another people in their place? Is this grace or is it patronage?

From the point of view of the Psalmist and the authors of this and similar passages of the Hebrew

Bible, there is no question that God's grace is limited to God's people, the descendants of Abraham and Sarah, the Chosen. From their point of view, everything good that happens to the Israelites is due to God's love of them, and everything bad is due to God's being angry with them for not doing what God demands of them.

This is far from the grace we are exploring in this book. In fact, this idea of a partisan God flatly contradicts the God of grace whose presence we see elsewhere in Torah. Worse, it denies the infinite nature of God's grace and therefore denies the fundamental notion that God is the source of all being. As such, it might even be understood as idolatrous, equating the grace of God with the good of the state.

Grace or Propaganda?

How, then, are we to reconcile God's seemingly partisan actions with our understanding of grace? I can think of only two ways.

First, we may dismiss the idea of God and gods altogether, insist that the Hebrew Scripture is nothing more than the work of Israelite propagandists seeking to explain, excuse, and celebrate Israelite history, no matter how bloody, and then state emphatically that what the Israelite authors call God's grace is simply history going their way. In this case, God is nothing but a figment of the Israelites' imagination, a character in a narrative designed to promote their status in their own eyes and the eyes of the world. It is at best historical fiction, and God is an invented character rooted in political expediency and military necessity.

What works with this option is that it erases our moral dilemma of a partisan God. Of course God is partisan; God is simply a partisan character in a partisan fiction. It isn't that God chose the Jews, but that the Jews invented a god who chose the Jews. God's slaughter of Israel's enemies is simply hyperbole used to muster the troops and the people who support them in whatever ventures the kings who commission these "histories" have in mind. Or, to put it more bluntly: the Bible is political propaganda created to serve the desires of Israelite political and priestly elites.

The problem with this approach to Hebrew Scripture is that it leaves Judaism without merit. If *YHVH* is only a figment of the Jewish imagination, then Judaism isn't what it claims to be: divine revelation. If Judaism is only the collective myths, memories, and mores of the Jewish people, it has no relevance beyond that people. This reduction of Judaism's universal call for justice and compassion to a parochial vision of jingoistic self-aggrandizement not only does a disservice to centuries of Jewish thought, but also undermines the meaning of any Jewish future.

To use but one emotionally charged example: If God didn't choose the Jews and promise them the Holy Land, why in heaven's name are we willing to sacrifice a single Jewish life in its defense? If Israel is just one more land in which we Jews lived during our four thousand years of existence, why ask Jews to move to Israel when it is clear that most Jews would be better off in New York, Los Angeles, or the Silicon Valley?

If we adopt this approach, then we need not maintain Judaism at all, and a book about God's grace is simply a guide to Jewish literary fiction. While I have no doubt that much of the Hebrew Bible is fiction, and even that which is fact is often spun in service to the Jewish narrative of the Chosen People in the Promised Land, I think there is more to Judaism and the Jewish idea of grace than the mere rationalization of jingoism and genocide. This book is about that something more. So let's move on to option two.

Beyond Good and Evil

Let me admit from the start that this option is not going to be easy for many to accept, but it is, in my opinion, not only a more viable option but a more credible one as well. Rather than dismiss God as a figment of our imagination or reduce grace to a divine carrot earned after succumbing to a no less divine stick, we could, and I suggest we must, redefine grace so that it includes not only blessing but curse, not only good but evil, not only what we desire but what we fear the most.

As long as we restrict grace to goodness and restrict goodness to what is good for the Jews, we miss the larger implications of *chesed,* God's grace. Grace is *tov,* and *tov* means "complete unto itself." God's grace isn't good or bad, but that which transcends good and bad. And what is true of God's grace is true of God as well. God is beyond good and evil. God isn't moral or immoral, but amoral.

While this may sound shocking, it isn't illogical. Good and evil only make sense from a human perspective. In this I follow Spinoza:

> By good I here mean every kind of pleasure, and all that conduces thereto, especially that which satisfies our longings, whatsoever they may be. By evil, I mean every kind of pain, especially that which frustrates our longings. We in no case desire a thing because we deem it good, but, contrariwise, we deem a thing good because we desire it: consequently we deem evil that which we shrink from; everyone, therefore, according to his particular emotions, judges or estimates what is good, what is bad, what is better, what is worse, what is best, and what is worst.

> (ETHICS 3, Prop 39)[3]

Good is what brings humans pleasure; evil is what causes us pain. Since God is beyond pleasure and pain, God is beyond good and evil. Being God means that God manifests both good and evil, for God is without limit.

If God is God, that is, if God is infinite, then good and evil must be a part of God and yet in no way defining of God. God cannot be identified with one aspect of the whole, but only with the whole itself. This is what the prophet Isaiah is saying to us when he has God say, "I form light and create darkness, I make good and create evil—I, *YHVH,* do all this" (Isaiah 45:7). This same point surfaces in the quote from Deuteronomy we discussed in chapter 1:

> I summon earth and sky to witness this day that I place before you living and dying, blessing and cursing. Now choose life that both you and your descendants may live.

> (DEUTERONOMY 30:19)

This, I suggest, is the purest expression of unconditional and unconditioned grace. First, it is freely given; there is no reason for God to place life and death, blessing and curse before the people. Second, it withholds nothing: both life and death are given, both blessing and curse are set forth. Third, it removes God from the equation of who gets what. God provides us with everything; it is up to us to do with it as best we can.

Grace, God's free-flowing, unconditioned, and unconditional love, is given to all beings without strings, and what is given is reality itself: life and death, blessing and curse. God is reality; God manifests all things and their opposites. God doesn't choose who gets life and who gets death; God simply sets both in motion, and we reap all that is given. God has no choice in this: the infinite cannot be less than infinite, and the only choice that we humans have is what we do with what we receive.

Upholding the Covenant

This brings us to the hardest point in our understanding of the covenant. Not hard to understand, but hard to do. If God is unconditioned and unconditionable reality, and God's grace is no less unconditioned and unconditionable, then there is no reason to praise one act of grace and condemn another. On the contrary, if we understand the message of Isaiah and Deuteronomy, we must respond with the wisdom of Job: "Shall we not accept the good as well as the bad from God?" (Job 2:10).

As I continue to remind you over and over lest you fall back into some other more comfortable and comforting definition of grace, *chesed* is the unconditional love of God manifesting as reality itself: life and death, prosperity and adversity, blessing and curse. The covenant with God is therefore a partnership with life and all life brings. Our covenant is this: God gives us reality, and we struggle to navigate that reality with compassion, justice, and love.

While there are no conditions placed on God's grace, there are consequences resulting from what we do with the grace we receive. We have seen them before. If we act wisely—if we do justly, embrace kindness, and walk humbly—we and the earth prosper (Deuteronomy 11:13–15); if we act poorly—if we perpetrate injustice, cruelty, and narcissism—we and the earth suffer (Deuteronomy 28:15, 28:18, 28:24). If we act wisely, "swords will be beaten into plowshares, and spears into pruning hooks; nations will no longer lift up swords against nations, and none will study war, and all will sit under their own vines and their own fig trees, and no one shall make them afraid" (Micah 4:3–4). If we act poorly, "foreign nations will swoop down like eagles ... slaughtering your elders and your infants, your herds and your harvests, leaving you with nothing.... Your defenses will crumble and you will be forced by starvation to cannibalize your own children ... (Deuteronomy 28:49–53).

God's grace is nothing less than reality as a whole and the freedom to engage it wisely or foolishly. The *brit*/covenant God made with humanity is not a quid pro quo compact, but a grace-filled act of creativity. God graced us with life. When we act in accordance with that gift, life functions as it should:

> Everything in this world has its moment,
> a season of ripening and falling away:
> Moments of birthing and moments of dying;
> moments of planting and moments of reaping.
> Moments of killing and moments of healing;
> moments of demolition and moments of building.
> Moments of weeping and moments of laughing;
> moments of mourning and moments of dancing.

Moments of scattering stones and moments of
 gathering stones;
moments of embracing and moments of distance.
Moments of seeking and moments of losing;
moments of clinging and moments of releasing.
Moments of tearing and moments of mending;
moments of silence and moments of talking.
Moments of loving and moments of hating;
moments of warring and moments of
 peacemaking.

(ECCLESIASTES 3:1–8)

It isn't that life lived well is all bliss. On the contrary, it is what life always is: everything and its opposite. What life well lived lacks is the unnecessary suffering caused by humans living foolishly. There will be moments of killing, but no mass murders; there will be wars, but no genocides. Life includes death, but life well lived isn't defined by it.

My point is this: God's grace places before us a world that can and will yield blessing and curse, life and death. We cannot have one without the other, but we can minimize the negative and maximize the positive if we live graciously, that is, if we live justly, compassionately, and humbly and thus align ourselves with our true nature as the alter ego of God.

Think in terms of an electric light socket. Plug a lamp into it and you get light; stick your finger into it and you're dead. Electricity doesn't choose your fate, you do. It is the same with God. God has manifested a world filled with grace. Plug into it wisely—with justice and compassion—and you will benefit by actualizing your potential as the image of God and becoming the likeness of God and a bearer of God's light. Plug into it foolishly—living unjustly and cruelly—and you will bring unnecessary suffering to yourself and the world around you. God doesn't reward one way of life and punish another. God has simply established the world in such a way that blessing and curse will follow naturally from the choices we make: "I place before you living and dying, blessing and cursing. Now choose life that both you and your descendants may live" (Deuteronomy 30:19).

Chapter 5

Grace & Forgiveness

Grace is not a bargain. Grace has no prerequisite: we neither deserve it nor earn it. Grace flows from God because grace is the nature of God. And because God is what is, God's grace flows naturally into even the narrowest nook and cranny. Yes, you can ignore the gift of grace, you can refuse to unwrap it, but you cannot avoid having it dropped off at your doorstep. Grace no less than sin crouches at the door (Genesis 4:6–7). And because grace and sin are both given, forgiveness, too, is part of the package.

On Sin and Forgiveness

Let us begin our exploration of grace and forgiveness by examining the nature of sin as defined in selections from two psalms: 32 and 51.

Happy are those whose *pesha* is forgiven,
whose *chata'ah* is buried.
Happy are those to whom *YHVH* assigns no *avon,*
and in whose spirit there is no deceit.

(PSALM 32:1–2)

I have left three key words in this section of Psalm 32 in their original Hebrew because they are too easily glossed over by the English word "sin." In Hebrew each word refers to a unique category of sin. *Avon* corresponds to deliberate or premeditated sin; *pesha* (or *fesha)* refers to inadvertent sin, sin that happens because one is thoughtless in one's actions; and *chata'ah* refers to the unintended negative consequences arising from a deliberate act intended for good.

You don't earn the gift of forgiveness of *avon, pesha,* and *chata'ah,* but you must unwrap it to benefit from it, and to do this you have to realize and admit that you have sinned. "While I kept silent, my body shriveled because of my suffering" (Psalm 32:3), but as soon as "I admitted my mistakes *[chata'ah]* to You, and no longer hid my wickedness *[avon],* and vowed to confess my thoughtlessness *[fesha],"* You forgave me (Psalm 32:5).

Forgiveness is an act of grace, and grace is the free-flowing love of God, so how is it that forgiveness is withheld until you confess? The answer is this: until you realize that you need forgiveness, you will not notice you already have it. This becomes both clearer and more problematic when we look at Psalm 51:

> Scrub me clean of my *avon,*
> and wash away my *chata'ah.*

My *fesha* and *chata'ah* are always in front of me.
Against You alone have I sinned *[chata'ah]*
And committed acts You deem evil....
I was born guilty,
My guilt began in the womb....
You desire truth in my innermost being,
So instruct my secret heart in wisdom.

(PSALM 51:4–8)

It seems inescapable that the Psalmist is saying that we are sinful from conception and hence born guilty, something many Christians are more than willing to concede, but something that most Jews reject. We read something similar in Genesis when God admits that every inclination of a person's heart is evil from childhood (Genesis 8:21). The ancient Rabbis took this to mean from birth.

Emperor Antoninus asked our Teacher [Rabbi Judah haNasi], "When does the evil inclination enter a person?" Rabbi Judah replied, "From the point of being an embryo." Antoninus objected, saying, "If so, the baby would dig through the womb and emerge prematurely." Rabbi Judah agreed, changed his mind, and said, "A person's heart is evil from childhood" (Genesis 8:21), which means from the moment of birth.

(GENESIS RABBAH 34:11)

So is it true that we are born in sin and with sin? If you imagine evil to be genetic in nature, if you imagine it is in our very DNA, then yes, we are sinners from the moment of conception. But this doesn't seem to be the way Rabbi Judah understood it at all.

Antoninus objects to Judah's original notion that sin comes with conception, and Judah accepts his objection and changes his mind. If evil originates with conception, Antoninus says, the embryo would dig its way out its mother's womb. Why? Because what Antoninus and the Rabbis meant by evil was selfishness run amok. A selfish embryo would have no patience for the birthing process and no concern about the welfare of its mother. Knowing nothing of the nature of things, it would impulsively tear the mother to shreds in its search for personal liberation from her womb. Since this doesn't happen, selfishness must arise later, perhaps at birth.

While both Antoninus and Rabbi Judah agree on this point, I would object, saying to them both, "The Hebrew you are taking for birth is *na'ar,* which means 'youth,' or as I would put it 'adolescence.' What Torah is telling us is that with the full arising of the self comes the dangerous inclination toward selfishness." I have no idea if Antoninus and Judah would agree and change their minds on this issue, but it does allow us to deepen our understanding of grace.

If the potential for sin is endemic to human nature—arising at conception or birth or with the coming of adolescence—it cannot be avoided. If it cannot be avoided, forgiveness is essential; that is, if I cannot help but sin, I cannot help but place myself at the mercy of God in my pursuit of forgiveness. If I cannot avoid sinning (in at least one of the three categories: intentional, inadvertent, and accidental) any more than I can avoid breathing, there is either forgiveness or damnation, with no middle ground between them. This is what Saint Paul argued in the early decades of Christianity, but for him forgiveness required the death of God's Son, whereas for Jews it requires only the acceptance of our having sinned.

Awakening to Forgiveness

It is our nature to sin—intentionally, inadvertently, accidentally—and because we cannot change our nature, we cannot avoid sin. The way to forgiveness only requires us to admit our condition. As long as we remain silent, as long as we deny the darker side of our nature, we are left groaning in the dark shadows of self-deception: "While I kept silent, my body shriveled" (Psalm 32:3). But as soon as we admit the truth of our nature, confessing not only to specific sins but to the fact that we have a dark side, then forgiveness happens of its own accord: "Then I admitted my sin to You, and no longer hid my iniquity ... I said, 'I will confess my transgressions to *YHVH,'* and You forgave..." (Psalm 32:5).

Notice that the Psalmist attests to no change in behavior. He doesn't say it was when he turned from his evil ways and made amends and lived an upright life that God forgave him. All that is needed to receive God's forgiveness is to admit the need for it. Not even ask for it—the Psalmist doesn't do that—just admit the truth.

This makes perfect sense. In their discussion of sin, Rabbi Judah explains to Antoninus that the Hebrew *mine'urav,* which Judah takes to mean "birth" and which I have taken as "adolescence," literally means "from his awakening" *(Genesis Rabbah* 34:10). Following this literal reading, we might argue that unless and until we awaken to our own shadow side, we are incapable of realizing we have sinned and instead take our behavior to be for the good.

Consider this for a moment. Think about the most horrendous act of human evil you can imagine—Hitler's slaughter of the Jews perhaps—and then look to see if it was cloaked in anything but positive terms. Here, for example, are selections from a 1941 essay and radio address by Joseph Goebbels, Hitler's minister of propaganda:

> All Jews by virtue of their birth and their race are part of an international conspiracy against National Socialist Germany. They want its defeat and annihilation, and do all in their power to bring it about....

> We wanted to make them visible as Jews, particularly if they made even the least attempt

to harm the German community. It is a remarkably humane measure on our part, a hygienic and prophylactic measure to be sure that the Jew cannot infiltrate our ranks unseen to sow discord....

That is an elementary principle of racial, national, and social hygiene.... The Jews are a parasitic race that feeds like a foul fungus on the cultures of healthy but ignorant peoples. There is only one effective measure: cut them out....

If we Germans have a fateful flaw in our national character, it is forgetfulness. This failing speaks well of our human decency and generosity, but not always for our political wisdom or intelligence. We think everyone else is as good-natured as we are....[1]

At no time does Goebbels call the German people to acts of evil. Rather he calls them to social hygiene. My point isn't to get into the thick of Nazi propaganda, but to suggest that there is no evil we can do that we cannot couch in positive terms. And as long as we do this, we maintain the lie that we have no dark side and that what we do is good.

What Torah is telling us is this: unless and until we admit to having a dark side, we cannot accept the already given grace that is God's forgiveness. And the way we admit to having a dark side is by confessing our sins. The two are in fact one. A sin is not a sin if, by definition, I have no dark side and am therefore incapable of sinning. A sin is only a sin if I have the capacity to sin and therefore admit to having a dark side. This is why Torah says that sin arises with awakening; awakening to our true nature, awakening to the fact that we have both *Yetzer haRa,* a shadow side capable of acts of selfishness and great evil, and *Yetzer haTov,* a good side capable of acts of selflessness and altruism.

As soon as we reach this state of awakening and confession, God forgives us (Psalm 32:5). This is not an "if–then" proposition. We do not earn God's forgiveness by achieving the state of awakening/confession. Rather awakening, confession, and forgiveness are all of a piece. And because of this, we can say that forgiveness is an attribute of divine grace.

We can see this "of a piece" nature of sin and forgiveness in the text of the *Avinu Malkeinu* (Our Father, Our King), one of the central prayers of the Jewish High Holy Day liturgy.

Avinu Malkeinu

> Our Father, our King, we have sinned before You ... have compassion on us and on our children ... bring an end to disease, violence, and starvation ... bring an end to strife and oppression ... inscribe us in the Book of Life, inscribe us in the Book of Redemption ... inscribe us in the Book of Forgiveness....

Read this prayer carefully and you will see that the reason for being inscribed in the Books of Life, Redemption, and Forgiveness (among others) is because we have sinned and not because we have repented our sins! In other words, forgiveness is an act of pure grace. We don't deserve it. We have done nothing to earn it. All we have done is admitted that we have sinned—and that is enough! Don't imagine that confession *triggers* forgiveness, but rather that confession and forgiveness arise together in the moment of awakening; the moment we become aware of our evil is the very moment God forgives us that evil.

In his marvelous compendium of teachings on the High Holy Days, Shmuel Agnon offers us this teaching called "The Feast at the Close of Yom Kippur":

> Let every man set his table and eat joyfully and with a good heart, as on a night when a holiday is hallowed, for on this day all his transgressions are forgiven, the mercy *[chesed]* of the Lord being with him. The same is written in the Midrash: "At the close of Yom Kippur a voice issues from heaven and says: 'Go thy way, eat thy bread with joy, and drink thy wine with a merry heart; for God hath already accepted thy works' (Ecclesiastes 9:7); and your prayer has been heard" (Ecclesiastes Rabbah III).[2]

A person is supposed to eat joyfully at the close of Yom Kippur because on Yom Kippur all sins are forgiven. What is the cause of this forgiveness? The mercy of God is with you. In Hebrew the word "mercy" is *chesed,* grace. In other words, forgiveness happens because God's grace is with you. The midrash Agnon cites makes this even more radical.

The original text of Ecclesiastes on which the midrash is based urges us to eat our bread in gladness and drink our wine with joy because eating bread and drinking wine are actions approved by God (Ecclesiastes 9:7). The midrashic use of the text in *Ecclesiastes Rabbah* 3 shifts the focus away from eating and drinking as prescribed actions and asserts that our eating and drinking are reactions to God having made peace with our prior actions, the sinful actions we confessed to during the High Holy Days. In other words, there should be no doubt in our minds that we are forgiven even though we have no new behaviors to present to God in order to earn this forgiveness.

Teshuvah, Tefillah, Tzedakah

This reading of forgiveness as grace received rather than as a benefit earned may seem to some to fly in the face of yet another central prayer of the High Holy Days:

> On Rosh Hashanah will be inscribed and on Yom Kippur will be sealed how many will die and how many will be born; who will live and who will die; who will die at their predestined time and who before their time; who by water and who by fire, who by sword, who by beast, who by famine, who by thirst, who by storm, who by plague, who by strangulation, and who by ston-

ing. Who will rest and who will wander, who will live in harmony and who will anxious, who will enjoy tranquility and who will suffer, who will grow poor and who will grow rich, who will be degraded and who will be uplifted. But repentance, prayer, and charity remove the stern decree.

Philosophically this is a difficult prayer to comprehend. The idea seems clear enough: God is about to determine humanity's fate for the coming year: so many will die and so many will be born. But what about the next line: who will die at their predestined time and who before it? How can this be?

If you are predestined to die on a specific date, how can you die on another date, earlier or later? The whole point of predestination is that the moment of your death is fixed and there is nothing you can do about it. If you can die before your time, there is no such thing as predestination.

The prayer continues with a list of horrible ways to die and then follows that list with a series of other options fate may have in store for you. You seem to have no control over any of this. You will live or you will die, and if you die, here are some of the ways it may happen, and if you live, here are the scenarios laid out for you. It is frightening, and it is meant to be. This is why the prayer ends the way it does—with a loophole: "But repentance, prayer, and charity remove the stern decree." Makes sense, except that the Hebrew text and the English translation don't jibe at all. The Hebrew references *teshuvah, tefillah,* and *tzedakah* as ways of softening one's fate; the English speaks of repentance, prayer, and charity. These are not the same.

"Repentance" in Hebrew is *charatah* and, like its English equivalent, implies a change of heart stemming from a feeling of guilt. One who repents becomes a new person, one who does *teshuvah,* literally one who returns, returns to an original state, becomes, if you will, not a new person but his or her original person.

Teshuvah means to return to your original nature, return to being the image of God (Genesis 1:27), God's alter ego, the sheath of godliness, the Light-bearer and vehicle for God's grace. This original nature is the awareness that you are light and shadow, good and evil, just as God is light and shadow, good and evil (Isaiah 45:7). Returning to your divine nature doesn't put an end to your capacity for evil, but removes all rationalization that masks such evil in the guise of good. Without rationalization you are forced to face the truth and take ownership of your dark side. And doing so is always accompanied by forgiveness.

The English word "prayer" in this context implies asking God to forgive your sins. In Hebrew this is called *bakashah,* "entreaty," not *tefillah,* the actual Hebrew word used in the liturgy. *Tefillah* is the noun form of the verb *hitpallel,* "to observe oneself." What softens the stern decree is returning to your original nature *(teshuvah)* through self-observation *(tefillah).*

You aren't being told to beg God to forgive you; you are urged to return to your original nature by carefully observing your self and your deeds. When you observe yourself, you realize that you can do good and you can do evil, and you go about the task of maximizing the former while minimizing (though never eliminating) the latter. But more profoundly you realize your true nature as *adam/adom,* God's alter ego. This is how *tefillah* links with *teshuvah* and is one way of achieving it.

In our English translation the third element of our loophole, "charity," comes from the Latin *caritas,* "heart," and implies an emotional component that the actual Hebrew, *tzedakah,* lacks. *Tzedakah* comes from *tzedek,* "justice." We engage in acts of generosity not because we feel like doing so, but because when we become self-aware *(tefillah)* and return to our true nature *(teshuvah),* we naturally act justly and understand that to act otherwise is contrary to that nature. While the potential for evil still exists, the actualization of evil is minimized with the realization of our truest nature as God's alter ego.

Yet even if *teshuvah, tefillah,* and *tzedakah* differ from "repentance, prayer, and charity," they still seem to function as a loophole, as a way to avoid our destiny and the consequences of our actions. Let me suggest otherwise: *teshuvah* is to return to what is, *tefillah* is to observe what is, and *tzedakah* is to act from what is, and none of this is about changing what is. What softens is not the stern decree, but our response to it.

People are still going to die, and some of them die horribly. People are still going to live, and some them live horribly. Nothing changes. You still have no idea into which category you fall. Life and death are still happening. The holy and the horrible still play themselves out in the lives of the innocent and the guilty alike. Nothing has changed but you.

By returning to your true nature, you realize that life and death are a matter of grace over which you have no control whatsoever, so any desire to make things other than they are disappears. By observing yourself, you can see when you are slipping out of that true nature and into the egoic self that seeks to control life and the lives of others. When you see this happening, return to and engage life from your true self. And when you do, you will act justly and with compassion regardless of what fate has in store for you.

In short *teshuvah, tefillah,* and *tzedakah* lead you to a state of radical acceptance. You come to realize that things are as they are because they could not be otherwise, and this softens your heart. If things happen because the conditions that require them to happen are present, there is no point in lauding or blaming; there is no point in getting angry or throwing tantrums. All we can do is accept what is as it is, engage what is graciously, and move on to encounter what is next.

Chapter 6

Grace & Faith

The Hebrew word for "faith" is *emunah.* We first encounter the word in Genesis 15:6. God promises Abram an heir, but Abram has no children and plans to make his servant, Eliezer of Damascus, his heir. God warns him not to do this and again promises Abram an heir. God leads Abram outside to look at the stars:

> God said, "Look to the sky and count the stars, if you can." Then God said to Abram, "Your descendants shall be no less numerous." And he [Abram] had faith in *YHVH;* and *YHVH* took this as a sign of Abram's righteousness.
>
> (GENESIS 15:5–6)

In this context the Hebrew word *emunah,* "faith," is linked to the English word "trust." Later in Torah, faith as trust is linked with steadiness:

> Then Amalek came and fought with Israel at Rephidim. Moses said to Joshua, "Choose some men and tomorrow take the battle to Amalek. I will stand on the top of the hill with the staff of God in my hand." So Joshua did as Moses told him and fought with Amalek, while Moses, Aaron, and Hur went up to the top of the hill. Whenever

Moses held up his staff, Israel prevailed; and whenever he lowered it, Amalek prevailed. But Moses's arm grew tired, so Aaron and Hur took a stone and put it under him that he might sit on it. They each held up his arms, one on one side, and one on the other side; so his hands were steady *[emunah]* until the sun set. And Joshua defeated Amalek and his people with the sword.

(EXODUS 17:8–13)

Isaiah 7:9 and 2 Chronicles 20:20 make use of this link between faith and firmness when they say, "If you do not stand firm in faith *[ta'aminu],* you will not stand *[tei'ameinu]* at all" and "Believe *[ha'aminu]* in *YHVH* your God and you will be made firm in your faith *[tei'ameinu ha'aminu],"* respectively. *Emunah* isn't faith in an idea, but firmness of action rooted in trust in God.

God, too, is said to have faith, and God's faith is demonstrated by the constancy, faithfulness if you will, of creation. For example:

From generation to generation
I will sing of *YHVH's* grace *[chasdei YHVH],* and proclaim
your [God's] faithfulness *[emunat'cha];*
I declare your grace *[chesed]* is confirmed,
the sky attests to your faithfulness *[emunat'cha].*

(PSALM 89:2–3)

My faithfulness and My grace shall be with him
[the Psalmist].

(PSALM 89:25)

It is good to give thanks to *YHVH,*
to sing praises to Your Name, High One;
to declare Your grace *[chasdecha]* each morning
 and
your steadfastness *[emunat'cha]* each evening.

(PSALM 92:2–3)

For *YHVH* is good,
His grace everlasting, and
His faithfulness endures in every generation.

(PSALM 100:5)

The linking of *emunah* and *chesed,* steadfastness
and grace, furthers the argument that for Judaism
God's grace is unconditional. God's faithfulness manifests as creation, creation is an expression of God's
grace, and since creation is creation for all regardless
of merit, God's grace is unconditioned and unconditional.

In his monograph, *The Place of Faith and Grace
in Judaism,* David Blumenthal writes:

Faith and grace are doubly reciprocal concepts. By this I mean that grace evokes faith and faith evokes grace; that acts of unmerited love call for acts of faithfulness, while acts of faithfulness call forth acts of unmerited love—in all dimensions of existence. Thus, God loves us in grace and we are faithful to Him, and vice versa: we are faithful to Him and He loves us in convenantal *[sic]* grace.[1]

While Blumenthal's argument hints at an "if–then" relationship between grace and faith, and thus one may imagine he is making God's grace conditional on humanity's faith, this hint is accidental and easily put to rest. Even if you argue that "grace evokes faith and faith evokes grace" the fact that each evokes the other makes the priority of one over the other moot. If each evokes the other, each is part of the other, and the two arise together. This is like our earlier metaphor of the magnet. A magnet has a positive and a negative pole, and you cannot have one without the other. Because this is so, you cannot say that one pole precedes the other and can only say that both poles arise together in the context of what it is to be a magnet. The same is true of grace and faith.

If grace and faith evoke each other, they must arise together, and if they arise together, they are in fact one in the same thing. Grace is faithful, steadfast, and trustworthy. And because it is steadfast and trustworthy, it is unconditioned and unconditional. Nothing can effect grace. Grace cannot be earned and hence cannot be lost. If you cannot merit receiving grace, you cannot merit losing grace either.

Yet, the more aware of God's *chesed* we are, the more we live with *emunah;* that is, the more we realize that all reality is a gift of divine grace, the more steadfast and trusting we are in our engagement with it. With this in mind, I agree with Blumenthal when he writes, "Faith and grace are of this world, in its mundaneness and in its crises. Faithfulness and unmerited love are incarnate in life, in its ordinariness and in its vicissitudes. Both have their origin in transcendence, but they have their real existence in immanence—in the here and now."[2]

Jonah and Job

What might it be to live with God's grace in the here and now? This is the question that shall occupy us for the rest of this chapter, and to answer it we will focus extensively on the messages found in two books of the Bible, each written between the sixth and fourth centuries BCE: the book of Jonah and the book of Job. Job is perhaps the Bible's quintessential person of faith. He is also, as I hope to show in this chapter, the Bible's greatest teacher of grace. The counterpart to Job is Jonah, and by comparing these two characters we begin to understand just what it is to live in grace with grace.

To place our analysis in context, let's take a moment to recap the key points I have made thus far: First, grace is God's unlimited, unconditional, unconditioned, and all-inclusive love for all creation. Second, God's grace cannot be merited; there is nothing you can do to earn God's grace. Third, because grace cannot be merited, it cannot be unmerited; there is nothing you can do that will prevent you from receiving God's grace. Fourth, God's grace manifests in life as life; your very existence, indeed the existence of all reality, is an expression of God's grace. Fifth, God's grace is, as Maimonides put it, "wily," that is, beyond good and evil, and hence capable of being experienced as good and evil. And sixth, God's grace is actualized when we realize the true nature of God as reality and the true nature of self as God-bearer, God's alter ego here on earth.

The Way of Jonah

The book of Jonah describes events that were said to have taken place during the reign of the Israelite king Jeroboam II (786–746 BCE). The book itself was probably written between 250 and 450 years after the events it describes. Jonah is one of the twelve Minor Prophets whose books appear in the Hebrew Bible. The term "minor" here has nothing to do with the importance of the books or their message, but refers to the shorter length of these books when compared to the longer books of the Major Prophets. The book of Jonah stands out among the Minor Prophets in that it doesn't contain prophetic statements per se but rather sets forth a narrative about Jonah himself.

The story of Jonah centers around a conflict between the prophet and God. God calls Jonah to go to Nineveh, the Assyrian capital, to warn the Assyrians that unless they repent (return to their true nature as *adam/adom,* God's alter ego), they will be destroyed. Jonah doesn't want to go. The Assyrians are Israel's enemies, and Jonah has no desire to save them. Instead, Jonah flees God, boarding a ship bound for Tarshish. Annoyed, God conjures up a storm at sea that threatens the lives of both Jonah and the crew.

Jonah informs the crew that the storm is his fault, and in an attempt to appease God, the crew throws Jonah overboard. A massive fish swims by and swallows Jonah. After three days and nights languishing in the fish's belly, Jonah acquiesces to God's command, and God has the fish carry him to Nineveh. Once there, Jonah obeys God's call to prophecy and convinces the Assyrians to heed God's warning. God forgives the Assyrians and in so doing enrages Jonah. You might recall that admitting sin is the key to discovering forgiveness. This is what the Assyrians do, thus proving the universality of God's grace. It is this very universality that enrages Jonah.

YHVH! Isn't this what I said would happen before I left my own country? This is why I fled to Tarshish in the first place: I knew you are a gracious God and merciful, slow to anger, and overflowing with infinite grace, always ready to forgive rather than punish. And now, *YHVH,* please take my life from me, for it is better that I die than live.

(JONAH 4:2–3)

It devastates Jonah's sense of justice to think that a people as wicked as the Assyrians, Israel's enemy to the north, can earn the grace of God. If God's isn't the exclusive property of the Chosen People, then Jonah wants no part of life.

Jonah's worldview is classic zero-sum: the world is composed of winners and losers, and for Israel to win, the Assyrians must lose. As Jonah perceives the world there is only so much grace and forgiveness to go around, and if Israel is to maximize its portion of these attributes, it must minimize the amount bestowed on non-Israelites such as the hated Assyrians. As a loyal son and prophet of Israel, Jonah fled from God in hopes of not having to be the instrument whereby Israel has to share the fixed pie of God's grace with others.

YHVH responds to Jonah's rant, asking, "Is your anger appropriate?" (Jonah 4:4). Jonah ignores God and builds a small shelter for himself east of the city. He waits inside to see what will happen to Nineveh. God then causes a large broad-leafed plant to spring up and further shelter Jonah from the sun. While Jonah says nothing to God, the story makes it clear that Jonah took comfort in the shade (Jonah 4:6).

The next morning God sends a worm to infect the plant. By the time the sun rises in the sky, the plant has withered and there is no sheltering shade. God then stirs up a hot easterly wind and has it blow in off the desert. The blazing sun and hot wind bring Jonah to the point of unconsciousness. In his delirium Jonah cries out to God, begging for relief in death: "I would rather die than live like this" (Jonah 4:8). God responds to Jonah, saying, "Are you that upset about the dead plant that you too wish to die?" (Jonah 4:9).

It is a strange question to ask. Jonah isn't complaining to God about God's failure to defend the plant against deadly insects; he is sensing that the heat is bringing him to the brink of death and wants God to end his suffering and kill him quickly. Jonah seems to ignore God's comment and repeats his desire to die. God continues to talk about the bush, hoping in this way to get Jonah to see the larger picture.

> Then *YHVH* said, "You didn't plant this bush or nurture it ... yet you are so concerned with it. If you can be so attached to this bush, should I not care about a metropolis such as Nineveh, in which live 120,000 people who don't know their right hand from their left? Not to mention their animals?"

> (JONAH 4:10–11)

These final words of the book of Jonah show a very different God from the God of the Flood, who destroys animals because of the sins of humans, and the God of Sodom, who is more than willing to slaughter the innocent along with the guilty. In those stories, it was God who had no feelings for animals and people; here it is Jonah who lacks empathy, while God recognizes that Assyrians and Israelites are both his children and that animals must not suffer on account of humanity's sins.

For our purposes, the key phrase is "people who don't know their right hand from their left." The Assyrians are incapable of knowing right from wrong, and God forgives them anyway. Even if they repent, how deep could their repentance be if they are so ignorant of the nature of things? Yet God forgives them not because they deserve it or earned it, but because God cannot help it.

Zero-Sum God; Zero-Sum World

Jonah is a stand-in for every person who imagines a zero-sum God and who lives in a zero-sum world. Living in a zero-sum world generates a deep sense of selfishness. People who live in such a world struggle with selfishness from their youth (Genesis 8:21). As soon as they are old enough to imagine that the pie is fixed in size and that if they want more others will have to get less, their imaginations turn to schemes that will benefit themselves at the expense of others. The God such people imagine is a zero-sum God whose grace and forgiveness are limited and must be earned.

Arriving in the Assyrian capital Jonah proclaims, "Forty days hence, Nineveh will be destroyed" (Jonah 3:4). The Assyrians take the prophecy seriously, and the king tears off his robe, replaces it with sackcloth, and sits repentant in ashes (Jonah 3:5–6). He then orders a nationwide fast, obligatory on people and animals, and commands everyone to turn from evil and injustice and to pray to God for forgiveness (Jonah 3:7–8).

> God observed the doings of the people, how they repented from their evil ways. And God changed course regarding the punishment planned for them, and did not carry it out.

> (JONAH 3:10)

The message of the book of Jonah is a bridge between the zero-sum theology of a God whose grace and forgiveness must be earned and the nonzero God whose grace and forgiveness are simply part of the divine nature.

What causes God's change of mind is the repentant behavior of the Assyrians. They have now earned God's grace and in so doing reflect a zero-sum worldview. Yet the very fact that Assyrians can merit God's grace is a radical idea in and of itself and suggests at least the beginning of a nonzero understanding of God. After all, they are Israel's enemies, and it would not be a shock to see God deal with them the way God dealt with the Egyptians, Hittites, Amalekites, and others who threatened Israel. But God forgives them, and in having God do so, the author of the book of Jonah is arguing for a universal nonzero God in opposition to the parochial zero-sum God worshipped by the more xenophobic among the Israelite people. But the author of Jonah is not done and pushes his view of God one step further, actually crossing the line from a zerosum God to a nonzero God.

In the third chapter of the book of Jonah the author tells us that God is motivated by the Assyrian change of behavior, but when God explains things to Jonah in 4:11 there is no mention of repentance at all. God simply loves the Assyrians as God loves all people and cannot bear to destroy them.

Using the death of the plant as his "teachable moment," the author of the book of Jonah links God's grace not to the behavior of others, but to the relationship of God to creation as a whole. In essence God says to Jonah, "Look how grieved you are over the death of this plant, and you had nothing to do with it at all. How can I, the Creator of all life, not be grieved over the fate of all life? How can I, Creator of humanity, not be grieved over the fate of humanity? My care and concern, my grief, causes Me to act gracefully."

Grace has nothing to do with merit or repentance, and everything to do with the simple fact that life comes forth from God and God cannot help but love it and be gracious to it. With Jonah as our baseline, let's move on to the story of Job, in which we discover a far deeper, and for some more troubling, understanding of God's nature and grace, and how we can live graciously as well.

The Way of Job

The book of Job is actually two books: an older prose story about a righteous man tested by God to see if he will hold fast to his trust/faith in God, and a later and far more lengthy poem that is inserted in the middle of the prose story. Stylistically the book of Job is a sandwich, with the poem stuffed between two slices of prose. It is the poem that explores the nature of reality and why bad things happen to good people. The book of Job stands out among the other books of the Bible in that it offers a radical departure from the standard "do good, get good; do bad, get bad" position that permeates so many biblical texts:

Tell the just, things will go well for them, for they will eat the fruits of their deeds. But woe to the wicked, for things will go ill for them, for what they have done to others will be done to them.

(ISAIAH 3:10–11)

But Er, Judah's firstborn, was wicked in *YHVH's* sight, and *YHVH* slew him.

(GENESIS 38:7)

No horror befalls the just, but the wicked are plagued by trouble.

(PROVERBS 12:21)

As comforting as such teachings may be, they rarely pan out in real life. The just often suffer, and the wicked often prosper. This more hard-edged truth is the truth the author of Job wishes to explore.

Here is my brief paraphrase of the original prose story:

Once upon a time in the Land of Uz there lived an upright and blameless man named Job who feared God and shunned evil. During a heavenly counsel meeting *YHVH* said to Satan, "Where have you been?" And Satan answered, "I've been on earth walking around."

"Did you notice my servant Job?" God asked. "There's no one as loyal to Me as him."

"Of course he's loyal," Satan replied, "you give him everything he wants: a good wife, fine children, and great wealth. Strip him of these, and he will curse You to Your face!"

"It's a bet, then," said *YHVH.* "Spare his health, but do what you wish with the rest." So Satan returned to earth to do as God decreed (Job 1:6–12).

Satan had Job's oxen and donkeys taken by marauding Sabeans (Job 1:15), his sheep and shepherds killed in a fire (Job 1:16), his camels stolen and his camel herders murdered by Chaldeans (Job 1:17), and his children killed when a tornado collapsed the house of their older brother with whom they were all dining (Job 1:18–19). But Job didn't curse God or blame Him. Rather he said, "I came into life naked, and naked shall I leave it; *YHVH* has given and *YHVH* has taken away; blessed is the name *YHVH*" (Job 1:21–22).

At the next counsel meeting *YHVH* taunted Satan, "Have you seen my servant Job? Though you incited Me against him, still he didn't curse Me!"

"That's because You spared him physical torment," Satan said. "Strike his body and he will curse You to Your face!"

God gave Satan dominion over Job's health, and Satan tortured Job's flesh with open sores and oozing wounds from head to heel. Job sat in ashes scratching his sores with jagged shards of broken pots. His wife cried out to him, "Do you still hold back? Curse God and die!" (Job 2:1–9).

But Job said to her, "You aren't a fool, woman, so why speak as one? Shall we not accept the good as well as the bad from God?" (Job 2:10).

Job's three closest friends heard of his suffering and came to comfort him. They sat with Job for seven days in silence, for his suffering was too great for words (Job 2:11–13). Job never lost his faith in God, and *YHVH* rewarded him for his loyalty and gave him more than what he had had in the past. And Job lived 140 years and died old and content (Job 42:10–17).

Between the arrival of Job's friends and the restoration of Job's fortunes the author of the book of Job composed and inserted a philosophical poem of some forty chapters. It is in the poem that we find the Way of Job and the deeper meaning of the book that bears his name.

Radical Acceptance

Before delving into the poem, however, let's spend some time on the older prose tale and what it has to say about grace. While the word *chesed* doesn't appear in this tale, Job's responses to suffering set up what I am calling the Way of Job. Here is the first one: "I came into life naked, and naked shall I leave it; *YHVH* has given and *YHVH* has taken away; blessed is the name *YHVH*" (Job 1:21).

We come into the world with nothing, and we leave it with nothing. Many centuries after the book of Job was written, Rabbi Elazar HaKappar taught, "Despite your wishes you were conceived, despite your wishes you were born, despite your wishes you live, and despite your wishes you die" *(Pirke Avot* 4:29). The condition of which Job and Rabbi Elazar speak includes even our will: we exist, we die, and we have no say in any of it. Blessed is the name *YHVH,* the One who is all birthing and dying.

Job asks nothing of God and receives whatever is given. He knows he didn't merit his good fortune any more than he merited his bad fortune. Fortune is all there is—sometimes good, sometimes bad—and as his second utterance makes plain, cursing reality is a waste of breath and the murmurings of fools: "You aren't a fool, woman, so why speak as one? Shall we not accept the good as well as the bad from God?" (Job 2:10). We receive everything from God, and everything means just that—everything. This is the way of radical acceptance. There is no choosing what will happen to us; there is only engaging what happens graciously.

Remember Deuteronomy 30:19: "I place before you living and dying, blessing and cursing. Now choose life that both you and your descendants may live." Job understands this. God places everything before us. It is up to us to choose. But wait! Did Job choose the horrors that befell his family and himself? On the contrary, Job chose life and blessing, and yet death and curses came upon him anyway. He chose life, and yet his children died. Was God lying to us in Deuteronomy? This is what the poetic chapters of the book of Job seek to find out.

Job's Friends: Blaming the Victim

Unlike their behavior in the original prose folktale, Job and his friends do not remain silent in the poem.

After seven days of silent mourning, Job breaks the silence and invites dialogue by cursing the day on which he was born (Job 3:3), wishing he had been stillborn (Job 3:16).

Job's friends, beginning with Eliphaz the Temanite, engage in what today we might call an intervention. Job is in denial. There's no need to curse the day of his birth, rather he must repent the quality of his life. God is good and God is just, and if Job is suffering—and he clearly is—it can only be because he is reaping the evil fruits of his wicked, albeit well-concealed, actions. A just God cannot act unjustly. Job's suffering must be deserved.

Unlike the readers of the book of Job, Eliphaz doesn't know that the cause of Job's suffering has nothing to do with Job at all, and everything to do with a bet between *YHVH* and Satan, so his argument for Job's guilt is understandable:

> Think now, who among the innocent has ever
> suffered?
> Who among the righteous was ever shunned?
> To my way of thinking, those who plow evil
> and plant wickedness harvest the same.
>
> (JOB 4:7–8)

Eliphaz believes in a just God who punishes the wicked only, and in a world in which only the evil suffer. If Job is suffering, his suffering is a punishment, and if it is a punishment, it is a just one. All Job need do is follow the example of the Ninevites in the book of Jonah: confess his sins and beg God to forgive him.

But we *have* read the prose introduction to this poem, and we know Eliphaz's argument is nonsense. Job isn't being punished but tested, and the test isn't for his own welfare but to see whether God or Satan will win a bet. You cannot read the book of Job without constantly returning to the opening scenes. The challenge of the book, and its promise, will be lost on you if you forget the real reason for Job's suffering.

Job, too, is ignorant of God's wager, and hence ignorant as well of the true cause of his suffering. Like Eliphaz, he too believes in a just God. "If only I knew that I suffered because of my sins," Job says, "this knowing would console me; I could even revel in my pain" (Job 6:8–10). But Job knows he is innocent and cannot follow Eliphaz's advice.

In addition to Eliphaz, Job's friends Bildad and Zophar also seek to comfort him, but they, too, believe Job is guilty. While they have no idea what Job may be guilty of, the more he insists on his innocence, the more harshly they berate him for not confessing his guilt.

Since Job is not moved by the rhetoric of these three friends, their younger companion, Elihu, seeks to soften the others' position while still protecting the idea that a just God can only do justly. According to Elihu, Job is wrong to question God's justice, and wrong to insist on his own innocence. God is gracious and merciful, ever ready to forgive if Job would but admit, if not guilt, at least the fact that he isn't perfect. Job doesn't disagree with Elihu the way he did with the others, but he is still not satisfied. He demands that God come and explain things to Job personally. Without warning, God does.

From the Whirlwind

God speaks to Job from the midst of a tornado (Job 38:1). While the book of Job is vague about this, I imagine Job suddenly surrounded by violent and swirling winds, with the voice of God speaking to him from everywhere at once.

As a reader who knows the true origin of Job's suffering, that is, God's wager with Satan, one might expect God to tell Job the truth, apologize to Job for his suffering, explain why it was necessary, and then reward him for helping God win the bet. But nothing of the sort happens at all. Rather than reveal the truth of Job's suffering, God reveals the truth of God's nature.

> Where were you when I laid the earth's
> foundations?
> Explain it to Me if you can!
> Did you fix its dimensions,
> or measure it with a line?
> Onto what foundation were its pillars sunk?
> Did you set its cornerstone

as the morning stars sang
and all the angels shouted with joy?
Did you shut the sea behind doors
when it rushed forth from its source?
Was it you who clothed it in clouds, wrapped it
in dense fog?
Did you establish breakers, barriers, and gates,
saying to the sea, "Come this far but no farther;
here your pounding waves will stop"?

(JOB 38:4–11)

Rather than tell Job the simple truth—"I made a bet with Satan"—God overwhelms Job with the enormity of divine power. This isn't an answer to Job, but a bald attempt to silence him. Or is it?

God ends this first round of self-revelation with an odd self-reference:"Shall one who should be disciplined complain against *Shaddai?* He who challenges God must respond" (Job 40:2). The divine name *Shaddai* appears thirty times in the book of Job. We have seen earlier that the divine name *Shaddai,* often coupled with *El* (God) as *El Shaddai* and translated as "Almighty God," may refer to God's life-giving properties. *Shaddai* is related to the Hebrew word for "field" and "breast." *Shaddai* is the fertile one, the nursing one, the life-giving one. Why would this be the name of the God who torments Job to win a bet?

The answer is that God is the Life-Giver, but the life God gives isn't always the life we want. The life God gives is the entirety of life: the good and the bad, which is what Job knows to be true of God from the very beginning, even in the prose prologue to the poem. We come into the world naked, we exit the world naked, and in between we receive the full fierce blistering spectrum of reality from blessing to curse.

Job's friends want to limit God to only one-half of the spectrum: God is just, and God's actions are just. But Job knows better. God isn't just; God is *Shaddai,* and *Shaddai* is beyond human categories of good and evil, just and unjust.

Job's mistake was to doubt his original intuition and to hold out for something less raw. Job, no less than his friends, wants God to conform to some form of human morality. Job cannot accept the lie that he is guilty of any wrongdoing, but neither can he accept the notion that God isn't just. There has to be an explanation, and God has got to provide it.

Job stays silent as God continues an exultant exposition of divine power. But eventually he is compelled to speak.

Job responded to *YHVH:*
I understand: I am nothing compared to You.
How can one of such of small worth answer You?

So I slap my hand to my mouth to silence speech.
I have spoken once, but I cannot answer You;
I tried a second time, but no more.

(JOB 40:3–5)

Having gotten his wish that God appear before him, Job is now hoping to make God go away. He is intimidated by the immensity of God and the enormity of God's power. Job isn't confessing to anything, just as God isn't confessing to anything. Job is simply saying that if the answer to the problem of the suffering of the innocent is that God can do whatever God wants, then Job is defeated and there is no longer a point to any further discussion with either God or Job's friends.

If Job were right in this, if God is simply trying to terrify Job into silence, the poetic portion of the book of Job would have ended with verse 40:5. The author could have then reverted to the prose story and given Job his reward for once again holding his tongue. But this isn't the author's point, and the book doesn't end just yet.

Job's Realization

God isn't satisfied with Job's silence. This isn't yet the *d'mamah dakah* (1 Kings 19:13), the sheer silence of spiritual awakening, but the faux silence of one who just wants to be left alone. God wants Job to awaken to a greater truth and so pushes Job toward the greater silence. The voice of God from the whirl-wind strips Job of his strategic silence and begins to question him all over again.

> *YHVH* answered Job from the whirlwind:
> Prepare yourself! Be a hero!
> I will ask; you will answer:
> Would you condemn My justice
> to maintain your innocence?

(JOB 40:6–8)

God goes on for another fifty verses, reaffirming God's power and making Job's lack of it all the more palpable. There is no development in God's argument. One verse doesn't lead logically to the next, and when God ceases to speak, God seems to do so arbitrarily. No point is reached, no argument is cinched, and no reference to the bet with Satan is even hinted at. It as if God simply tires of telling Job how awesome God is.

God's silence seems to compel Job to speak, and when he does, something has changed. The change is subtle and often lost in English translation, but it is crucial if we are to understand the message of Job and how the Way of Job teaches us to live with God's absolute and wily grace. To understand the point I am about to make, we must be familiar with the standard English translations of Job's final words to God.

Here's the translation from the Jewish Publication Society:

Job said in reply to the Lord:
I know that You can do everything,
That nothing you propose is impossible for You.
Who is this who obscures counsel without
 knowledge?
Indeed, I spoke without understanding
Of things beyond me, which I did not know.
Hear now, and I will speak;
I will ask, and You will inform me.
I had heard You with my ears,
But now I see You with my eyes;
Therefore, I recant and relent,
Being but dust and ashes.

(JOB 42:1–6, JPS)

And here's another, from the New Revised Standard Version of the Bible:

Then Job answered the Lord:
"I know that you can do all things,
 and that no purpose of yours can be thwarted.
'Who is this that hides counsel without
 knowledge?'
Therefore I have uttered what I did not
 understand,
things too wonderful for me, which I did not know.

'Hear, and I will speak;
I will question you, and you declare to me.'
I had heard of you by the hearing of the ear,
but now my eye sees you;
therefore I despise myself,
and repent in dust and ashes."

(JOB 42:1–6, NRSV)

Let's carefully unpack this final speech of Job. First, let's do away with the temptation to imagine that Job is supplicating himself before a gigantic King. Remember that the Bible never says "Lord," but *YHVH*, and *YHVH* isn't a person, a being, or even a Supreme Being, but be- *ing* itself. God is the is- *ing* of reality, the creativity of creation, the source and substance of all that was, is, and will ever be. God is *YHVH,* and *YHVH* is *Shaddai:* the birther of worlds and the breast that feeds them.

This is why the author of the book of Job has God appear to Job in a whirlwind. *YHVH* is ever moving, never fixed, and impossible to pin down physically or theologically. God isn't here or there; God is here and there and everywhere. The book of Job is using words to reveal a reality that is fundamentally beyond words, a reality that is best perceived in the realm of sheer silence where the zero-sum ego dies and the nonzero alter ego of God is found. So Job isn't addressing the King of Kings, but reality itself. What he is saying is this: "I understand now that You are doing everything.

There is nothing else but reality, and You are it. I also know that whatever is, is what it is because You are what You are. The will of God is the nature of God, and the nature of God manifests as the world and everything in it.

"I spoke without knowing this; I spoke of things I did not and could not understand. I sought to reduce You to me, but I see now that You are trying to expand me to You. I had listened to the priests and sages, and heard about You with my ears, but You are nothing like the notions they impart. Now my eye sees You—not the physical eyes, for they are blinded by the dust You swirl around me—but with my inner eye, my intuition, a knowing that I can neither reduce to words nor deny with words. A simple truth awakens in me: I am the very dust that is creation; I am the wildness, and in this I find comfort."

My version of Job's final words stretches the original, but I think it more accurately represents the meaning of the text than does the standard English translations. The traditional rendering of the words of Job, words of self-hate, self-loathing, words of a man groveling in the dirt, are false and misleading. In fact they undo the very message the author of the book of Job seeks to impart.

I Am Dust! And So Are You!

In Hebrew, Job's final words are *Al kein* (therefore) *em'as* (I recant) *v'nichamti* (and I am comforted) *al afar va'eifar* (about being dust). Nowhere in the Hebrew Bible does *em'as* mean "to despise oneself," though it can and does mean to humble oneself. The two are not the same. Enveloped in the whirlwind of God, the infinite is- *ing* of all creation, Job is humbled; he knows that his life is a small thing, a speck of wind-tossed dust, but that doesn't mean he despises it. On the contrary, his being dust is a comfort to him.

Notice that Job isn't kneeling in dust and ash as the NRSV would have us believe; he is realizing that he *is* dust and ash. This is the image given by the JPS translator. But the JPS translator misses the fact that this realization is comforting to Job. To see that this is the case, that Job is comforted by the realization of his own smallness, we must turn to another translator, Stephen Mitchell:

> I had heard of you with my ears;
> But now my eyes have seen you.
> Therefore I will be quiet,
> Comforted that I am dust.[3]

As Stephen Mitchell explains in the notes to his translation, the phrase *afar va'eifar,* "dust and ash," occurs only two other times in the Hebrew Bible—Job 30:19 and Genesis 18:27—and both times it refers to the human body. More importantly, the very fact that we humans are dust is the reason God has mercy on us—"God knows how we were formed, and remembers that we are dust" (Psalm 103:14)—and like a father, God has compassion on us (Psalm 103:13).[4] Our realization of our being dust is the key to our understanding the grace of God. Being dust, we are part of the swirling of God's creation, which is itself a manifestation of God's nature, God's exuberant and infinite grace.

The message of Job is that we are dust and dust is holy. We are divine not in spite of our physicality, but as an expression of physicality. We are *adam/adom,* the sheath of God, the bearer of God's light. Failure to realize the true message of Job goes hand in hand with a picture of humanity that is anything but grace-filled, as the following selection from the Yom Kippur liturgy reflects.

The Anti-Job

Raba on concluding his prayer added the following: My God, before I was formed I was not worthy [to be formed], and now that I have been formed I am as if I had not been formed. I am dust in my lifetime, all the more in my death. Behold I am before You like a vessel full of shame and confusion. May it be Your will, *YHVH* my God, that I sin no more, and the sins I have committed before You be wiped out in Your great mercies, but not through evil chastisements and diseases! This was the confession of R. Hamnuna Zuti on the Day of Atonement.

(Talmud, *Berachot* 17a)

This prayer continues to be part of the Yom Kippur liturgy, and hence the self-hatred mistakenly read into the book of Job continues to speak to us in our own time. This focus on self-defilement obscures the truth that in being dust we are one with creation, which is one with God and God's grace. We are dust, and as dust we are sheaths for divine light. This dust, this mortal body, is a light-bearer and a God-bearer and a grace-bearer.

When we realize our true nature as dust, we no longer seek, as did Job's friends, to impose arbitrary categories on reality. Rather we welcome and learn to live with the dynamic tension of life and death, blessing and curse, abundance and scarcity. This is what Job discovers by book's end and what we who read this book should discover as well.

Part Two

The Practice of Living Graciously

Chapter 7

Grace & the Ten Sayings

The *mitzvot* of Judaism are the way Jews live our true nature as God-bearers and take up the challenge of enlightening the world about the nature of creation as the exuberant and wily grace of God. The *mitzvot,* lived as vehicles for grace, become the way we become conduits for grace, and hence the "failure of any Jew to live up to the precepts of the Torah puts the entire universe at risk."[1]

Mitzvot have two purposes: (1) they are the mnemonic devices we have invented to continually remind ourselves of the true nature and responsibility of humanity, and (2) they are physical practices that engage us in the process of *teshuvah, tefillah,* and *tzedakah* (returning to our original nature through self-observation, and just and compassionate action), without which we would forget who we are as human beings and fail at our mission as bearers of divine light. To place *mitzvot,* the traditions and commandments of Jewish life, in the context of grace, we would, once again, be wise to summarize and restate the main points of this book:

1. God is what is; nature naturing; the source and substance of all reality.

2. God is intrinsically dynamic, be- *ing* rather than a being or even a Supreme Being.

3. God's be- *ing* manifests in time and space as creation.

4. You and I and all life are expressions of God the way sunlight is an expression of the sun.

5. Just as the sun embraces and transcends all of its rays, so God embraces and transcends all reality.

6. Grace is God's overflowing, infinite, and dynamic creativity manifesting as all possibility—life and death, blessing and curse, abundance and scarcity, and so on—and because it is so, it is called by Maimonides "wily," suggesting God's grace is beyond human categories and desires.

7. God's grace flows out to all beings, offering them the fullness of God's creativity—life and death, blessing and curse (which, again, speaks to its wiliness)—without protecting them from any of it.

8. The way to live with grace is the Way of Job, the way of radical acceptance that continually recognizes and takes comfort in the holiness of things and thus allowing us to open to the grace of God however it manifests.

9. Living with radical acceptance is best done through *teshuvah* (continually returning to the realization of our true nature as expressions of God), *tefillah* (self-observation in order to see when we are deviating from our true nature), and *tzedakah* (embracing life, however it manifests, with justice and compassion).

10. Within the context of Judaism, the *mitzvot* provide a system of behaviors designed to promote *teshuvah, tefillah,* and *tzedakah* and in so doing help us to recognize grace and live graciously.

There are 613 *mitzvot* in Judaism, and taking up each one in turn is out of the question. Ours is not an encyclopedic examination of Jewish practices as vehicles for gracious living. Rather, I will select only a few examples from the corpus of *mitzvot,* explore them from the perspective of grace, and then invite you to do the same with the others. Let's begin with the Ten Sayings.

Grace and the Ten Sayings

The word *chesed* never appears in the Ten Sayings. Interestingly enough, neither does the word "command" or "commandments." What we call the Ten Commandments the Hebrew Bible calls *Aseret haD'varim,* "the Ten Words" or "the Ten Sayings" (Exodus 34:28). The Septuagint, the third-century-BCE Rabbinic translation of the Hebrew Bible into Greek, also avoids the word "commandments," preferring *tous deka logous,* or "the Ten Words." In the

Talmud, the Rabbis too avoid "commandments" and speak of *Aseret haDibrot,* "the Ten Sayings." This is important because I intend to read the Ten Sayings not as commandments to be followed under some presumed penalty of law, but as guidelines as to what it is to live graciously in the midst of God's wild and wily grace.

Imagine God's grace as radio waves. As you read this book, the air around you is filled with broadcasts from radio stations both local and distant. Unless a radio is presently turned on and catching these waves and translating them into audible sound, you're oblivious to these broadcasts. If you turn on a radio, however, you have the potential to pick up whatever programming is already there. I say "potential" be-cause if you want to receive the broadcasts you have to tune your receiver to the proper frequency, and only when you do so do you have access to the signals that are present. Your radio doesn't create the signals, nor is having a radio a prerequisite for there being signals in the first place. The signals are broadcast freely. The radio only aligns with them.

The same is true of grace. God's grace is a given that is always being given. There is nothing you have to do, or can do, to merit this grace. Unless you are properly attuned to it, however, there is no way to experience it. The Ten Sayings are ways of fine-tuning your life so that you are aware of the grace that is being given.

Remember, God's grace is unconditional and un-conditioned. To attune yourself with it you too must move closer and closer to unconditionality as well. The *Aseret haD'varim* are ways of doing this. Let's see how.

In the Book of Leviticus we are told, "You shall keep My laws and My rules, by the pursuit of which man shall live: I am the Lord" (Leviticus 18:5, JPS). While not a misleading translation by any means, the standard JPS rendering fails to unleash the deeper meaning of the text. I choose to read it this way: "I am *YHVH,* the Life of all life. You can live graciously, and adhering to My rules and laws will help you do so." What my rendering seeks to make clear is that God's rules are designed to attune us to gracious living. The early Rabbis of the Talmud read this verse similarly: "You shall live by them, and not die by them" *(Yoma* 85b). And the living we are talking about is a living with the radical acceptance that comes with a full awareness of God's grace.

Here are the Ten Sayings as represented in the standard Jewish Publication Society English translation:

1

I the Lord am your God who brought you out of the land of Egypt, the house of bondage: You shall have no other gods besides Me.

2

You shall not make for yourself a sculptured image, or any likeness of what is in the heavens above, or on the earth below, or in the waters under the earth. You shall not bow down to them or serve them. For I the Lord your God am an impassioned God, visiting the guilt of the parents upon the children, upon the third and upon the fourth generations of those who reject Me, but showing kindness to the thousandth generation of those who love Me and keep My commandments.

3

You shall not swear falsely by the name of the Lord your God; for the Lord will not clear one who swears falsely by His name.

4

Remember the sabbath day and keep it holy. Six days you shall labor and do all your work, but the seventh day is a sabbath of the Lord your God: you shall not do any work—you, your son or daughter, your male or female slave, or your cattle, or the stranger who is within your settlements. For in six days the Lord made heaven and earth and sea, and all that is in them, and He rested on the seventh day; therefore the Lord blessed the sabbath day and hallowed it.

5

Honor your father and your mother, that you may long endure on the land that the Lord your God is assigning to you.

6

You shall not murder.

7

You shall not commit adultery.

8

You shall not steal.

9

You shall not bear false witness against your neighbor.

10

You shall not covet your neighbor's house: you shall not covet your neighbor's wife, or his male or female slave, or his ox or his ass, or anything that is your neighbor's.

(EXODUS 20:2–14, JPS)

Read this way it is difficult to see the link between the *Aseret haDibrot* and grace. What we need do is recast the commandments in the positive: rather than the conventional "You shall not...," start each command with "You can choose to...."[2] Read this way the Ten Sayings become guidelines of living graciously:

1. I am *YHVH* your God, the be-ing of all being, who liberates you from narrowness and entrapment.
2. You can choose to live without idols.
3. You can choose to live without uncritical thinking.
4. You can choose to live without endless consumption and toil.
5. You can choose to live without devaluing your elders.
6. You can choose to live without murdering.
7. You can choose to live without adultery.
8. You can choose to live without kidnapping.
9. You can choose to live without giving false testimony.
10. You can choose to live without coveting. (Exodus 20:2–14)

Clearly I have not limited myself to tweaking the Hebrew in service to a modern English rendering. Instead I have sought to articulate the core idea I believe each saying contains and have stated that idea in a positive manner that speaks to how it can be lived as an expression of divine grace. This will become evident as we take up each of the Ten Sayings in turn.

Living without Enslavement

The first saying reminds us what God is about: liberation. While standard English translations render this text as "I am the Lord your God who took you from the Land of Egypt, from the house of bondage," this is far too limiting. God is not simply that power that freed the ancient Israelites from captivity in Pharaoh's Egypt; God is that power that frees us from all bondage.

The Hebrew word *Mitzrayim,* accurately though too narrowly translated as "Egypt," is a pun. According to the standard Hebrew etymology, the root of the Hebrew word *mitzrayim* is *mem/tzadi/resh, metzeir,* meaning "to border," "to shut," or "to limit." Other etymological theories suggest that the origin of *Mitzrayim* lies with the Hebrew word *tzar,* meaning "straits," "distress," "narrow," and "tight," or *tzarar,* meaning "to bind," "to tie," "to restrict," or "to narrow." The prefix *mi* means "from." Regardless of the etymological theory you prefer, the end is the same: *Mitzrayim* is not simply the land of ancient Egypt but the state of being bound.

Living mindful of God's grace, living a gracious life of *teshuvah, tefillah,* and *tzedakah,* you are free from narrowness, entrapment, and slavery. And if you do slip into these, attune yourself with God and align yourself with the godly, and you will slip out of these as well.

We enslave ourselves when we fail to live the next nine commandments; when we invent gods who excuse our selfishness; when we engage in uncritical thinking and endless consumption; when we define human worth in economic terms; when we allow rage to boil over into murder, and sexual desire to violate the integrity of our relationships; when our hunger for things excuses theft and our anger at an other translates into false testimony against them; and when our desire to exceed our neighbors' success results in efforts to limit their success. The teachings that follow are ways in which we can attune and align ourselves with the greater reality of which we are a part and free ourselves from these enslavements.

Living without Idolatry

God is beyond anything we can imagine, and yet we cannot escape imagining. The key to this paradox is to never mistake our imaginings for truth. This is what the prophet Micah taught when he said that God requires but three things of us: "Do justly, act graciously [or love *chesed*], and walk humbly with your God" (Micah 6:8). Why "your" God rather than just "God"? Because God is unknowable, and what we claim to know and worship is our idea about God, literally a god of our own imagination.

Micah isn't telling us to abandon our ideas about God—this is probably not doable—but to treat all our ideas about God with humility. That is, we are never to mistake our ideas *about* God *for* God. We can hone our theologies as best we can, but in the end we have to take them with a grain of salt, and doing so frees us from becoming enslaved to them.

Living without Uncritical Thinking

The third saying, the prohibition against taking God's name in vain, is about using the name of God to validate a false statement. We do this all the time: "I swear to God, the check is in the mail"; "I swear to God I didn't take the money in your purse"; "If I'm lying about this, let God strike me down where I stand." Yet I think there is more to this teaching than that.

The more egregious entrapment is using the name of God to sanction evil. The Hebrew Bible is peppered with God-sanctioned acts of evil. In Deuteronomy, for example, Moses speaks with pride of God's deliverance of Sihon into the hands of the Israelites:

> *YHVH* our God gave him over to us; and we destroyed him and his children—all of his people. When we captured his towns, we slaughtered men, women, and children. We left no one alive.

(DEUTERONOMY 2:33–34)

Later in the same book the Israelites are commanded to commit genocide against the indigenous peoples living in the Promised Land:

> You must not let anything that breathes remain alive. You shall slaughter them all—the Hittites and Amorites, the Canaanites and Perizzites, the Hivites and Jebusites—just as *YHVH* your God commands.

(DEUTERONOMY 20:16–17)

And in the book of Joshua we learn that after the Israelite soldiers defeated and killed every last soldier of the town of Ai, "all Israelites," not only the soldiers, attacked noncombatants, murdering old men, women, and children:

> The men and women slaughtered that day totaled twelve thousand—the entire population of Ai. For Joshua did not restrain his hand, but stretched out the sword until he had utterly destroyed all the inhabitants of Ai.

(JOSHUA 8:25–26)

Did God actually sanction genocide? Of course not; God is reality, not a warlord, but Joshua needed a divine warlord to sanction his military campaign, so he conjured up the god he needed to get the people to do what he wanted. Joshua was not the first to imagine a god in whose name one can kill with impunity, nor was he the last. Open almost any newspaper today and you will read the exploits of contemporary Joshuas waging brutal war against their enemies in the name of their gods.

This is why it is to so vital that we hold our ideas of God humbly. Or, as Job showed us, this is why we must realize that an authentic encounter with God is humbling. Job meets the real God and is humbled and brought to the sheer and transformative silence central to spiritual awakening. Joshua invents his own god and is emboldened for war, drowning out any other option by substituting sheer silence with deafening propaganda.

Freeing ourselves from uncritical thinking frees us to enter the silence and question the commandments humans place in the mouths of their gods. In so doing we free ourselves from these zerosum gods and their evil commands, and free ourselves for the nonzero God and a life of justice, compassion, and peace.

Living without Endless Consumption and Toil

Of all the teachings in the Ten Sayings it may be the Sabbath that is the most essential to attuning our lives to grace and the grace-filled God. The Sabbath is a day for being rather than becoming, for celebrating life rather than earning a living. This is a day for hallowing what is rather than scrambling for what we imagine we must have. The Sabbath isn't a day for remembering freedom, but for living free.

Shabbat well-lived frees you from all idols, especially the god of work, who demands endless toil in service to endless consumption. The god of work insists living must be earned, whereas the God of grace gives life as a gift. The god of work insists that we are what we do for a living; the God of grace teaches that we are an expression of God's grace created with the capacity to become a vehicle for gracing others. The god of work never allows us to catch our breath; the God of grace encourages us to breathe easy and full. The Sabbath frees us from the god of work and attunes us to the God of grace.

The relationship of Shabbat to Judaism is too central to be left to such a brief summary, so we will devote chapter 8 to a fuller exploration of Shabbat and grace.

Living without Demeaning Elders

Honoring our elders isn't simply a matter of respecting the aged, but a challenge to see through the lie that the value of a human being is determined by his or her capacity to produce and add to the economy.

Today, no less than in ancient times, your worth is often dependent on your ability to contribute to the economy. In some societies it was customary to let the elderly who lacked the means to take care of themselves die. They were considered a drain on society because they could no longer contribute to its economic wellbeing.

What the Ten Sayings are teaching us is that the worth of a human being is dependent on nothing other than the fact that he or she is a human being made in the image of God. This is true if the person is wealthy or destitute, capable of working or in need of daily care. It doesn't matter, and because it doesn't matter, living a life that includes honoring the aged—that is, seeing to the welfare of those too old to be economically productive—is part of what it means to live a life of grace.

Living without Murder

Torah is not opposed to killing, and the sixth commandment doesn't expect us to refrain from killing, only from premeditated acts of homicidal violence against another human being. Why? Because such acts force us to imagine that the other we are planning to kill is worthy of death, less than human, less a manifestation of God's grace than we are.

Living without murdering requires that we live without demonizing others. Living without demonizing others requires that we see the other as a fellow human, and to realize the other to be a human being is to realize the other as an expression of

God, God's alter ego. To live without murdering is to live without blinding ourselves to the divine nature of the other. It is to live without the delusion that the other is somehow demonic. It is to live without the folly of zero-sum competition that assumes that my success depends on your failure. And living without all this nonsense is living with grace.

The teaching against murder can be linked with the next three teachings as well: just as we are capable of living well without taking another's life, we can also live without taking someone's trust, property, or reputation.

Living without Adultery

The only sexual relationship proscribed in the Ten Sayings is adultery because adultery is less about sex and more about trust. What is stolen in an adulterous relationship is the trust between partners. Living without adultery is living without breaking the bonds of trust with one's beloved.

We have seen how in Judaism trust is linked with faith, and both are linked with the notion of steadfastness. When we trust people, we have faith that they will say what they mean and do what they say. Living this saying is living a life of integrity, and living with faith, trust, and integrity is, once again, living with grace.

Living without Kidnapping

The actual Hebrew of this saying speaks of kidnapping rather than stealing. While few English translations render the Hebrew this way, this was how the teaching was understood in ancient times. In the Babylonian Talmud, for example, the Rabbis discuss the abduction of slaves, indentured servants, and children and ask one another to provide a biblical source to bolster a law against kidnapping:

> Rabbi Josiah said: From "Thou shall not steal" (Exodus 20:13). Rabbi Johanan said: From "They shall not be sold as bondsmen" (Leviticus 25:42). Now, there is no dispute between them, for the first states the prohibition against kidnapping, and the second states the prohibition against selling a kidnapped person into bondage.

> (TALMUD, *SANHEDRIN* 86a)

While the Torah has many prohibitions against theft, the Ten Sayings focus on kidnapping, or more accurately human trafficking, because this is the most egregious kind of thievery. As with the focus on murder rather than killing, the focus here is on kidnapping rather than theft because kidnapping (human trafficking), like murder, dehumanizes the other. Human trafficking reduces the human being to something less than human, in this case property.

What is being stolen is a person's very humanity. Broadly speaking there are many ways to do this short of literal kidnapping. We rob people of their humanity when we treat them as a commodity, when we make their inalienable rights contingent on wealth, race, gender, class, sexual preference, or whatever else we latch on to in order to devalue a person. But let us not rush to turn this saying into a metaphor when so many thousands of human beings are being abused through human trafficking, and we have such a long way to go before we have ended this horror. When we live without kidnapping, we live in a manner that honors another's inherent value and doesn't turn another into a commodity, and we participate in what it is to live with grace.

Living without Giving False Testimony

Like the previous teaching, the ninth saying is specific in its injunction: it is not lying per se that is prohibited, but lying in court under oath. Similar to the teaching not to use God's name to preclude critical investigation of an argument or political position or policy, the ninth saying precludes deliberately lying under oath to undermine the quest for truth in a court proceeding.

It is one thing to lie, saying, "I swear I was out with Jimmy at the bowling alley," when in fact Jimmy wasn't with you at all, and quite another to say under oath, "I swear it was Jimmy who robbed the bowling alley," when in fact it was you. While the former violates a bond of trust between two individuals, the latter corrupts the very foundation of a lawful society without which no lasting civilization can survive.

What the Ten Commandments prescribe in these areas are the minimum standards that make collective life possible. In this sense the Ten Commandments are to the social order what the opening chapter of Genesis is to the natural order; without each there is only a formless void. Whereas Genesis structures (and thereby creates) the physical world, the Ten Commandments structure (and thereby make possible) a social world. Regarding force ... you can bicker and fight, but killing ... will not be permitted, for it instigates blood feuds that shred community.... Similarly with sex. You can be a rounder, flirtatious, even promiscuous, [but] sexual indulgence of married persons outside the nuptial bond will not be allowed, for it rouses passions the community cannot tolerate.... As for possessions, you may make your pile as large as you please and be shrewd and cunning in the enterprise ... [but] you may not ... pilfer directly off someone else's pile, for this outrages the sense of fair play and builds animosities that become ungovernable.... Finally, regarding the spoken word, you may dissemble and equivocate, but there is one time when we require that you tell the truth, the whole truth, and nothing but the truth....[3]

Of course not all of us are called to testify in court, and if this saying is to be relevant to us all, it must be expanded. I suggest doing so this way: live without claiming an authority you do not possess. We hear people making false claims all the time: claims about evolution being a theory rather than a fact; claims about climate change having no relationship to human activity; claims that this product is good for you; claims that this politician did something that precludes election or reelection. And all these claims are backed up by sources that are biased at best, fallacious at worst. Living the ninth saying is speaking the truth and not merely your opinion about what the truth ought to be.

Living without Coveting

The last of the Ten Sayings seems to differ from all the others in that it refers to desire, feeling, rather than behavior. While controlling your actions is doable, controlling your feelings is not. After all, by the time you know you are feeling covetous or jealous of someone, the feeling is already present, and if the commandment is about feelings, it is already broken.

To get around this problem, the ancient Rabbis finessed the meaning of this teaching, understanding it to mean not that we are to avoid feelings of jealousy, but that we are to avoid acting on those feelings in a way that deprives our neighbor in order to satisfy ourselves. It is one thing to channel feelings of covetousness regarding your neighbor's new car into working hard to purchase a similar car for yourself, and quite another to allow those feelings to justify stealing your neighbor's car.

The tenth saying invites us to live outside a zero-sum frame of mind. That is, if you covet what your neighbor has, use that feeling to motivate yourself to work hard in order to secure something similar for yourself. This is nonzero thinking: your win isn't dependent on another's loss. In other words, living graciously means applying yourself to achieve your goals without robbing others of the opportunity to achieve their goals as well. This reading of the tenth saying allows the Ten Sayings as a whole to prohibit stealing as well as kidnapping and avoids our having to control our emotions, something few if any of us can do with any regularity.

***

The importance of the Ten Sayings in the context of grace is this: to live with grace we must see all life as an expression of grace. To see life in this way, we must free ourselves from those notions that lock us into a zero-sum worldview that makes God's grace contingent on our own prejudice and priorities. Living the Ten Sayings is living free from this zero-sum world and open to the nonzero world that is the expression of God's infinite grace.

Chapter 8

Grace & Shabbat

In the previous chapter we explored the Ten Sayings as principles by which you might construct a grace-filled life. In this chapter we will focus on Shabbat as another way of infusing your life with grace. We will begin with an exploration of Shabbat as an affirmation of divine grace and then offer some suggestions for making Shabbat a day of grace in your life.

According to the book of Genesis, God completed the work of creation on the sixth day, and "on the seventh day, having completed all the work that God had been doing, God ceased from all the work that God had done. Then God blessed the seventh day and hallowed it by ceasing from all the work that had been done" (Genesis 2:2–3). In chapter 2 we saw how creation itself was an act of grace; can it be that cessation from creative activity can be no less grace-filled?

Shabbat is mentioned in both versions of the Ten Sayings. In Exodus we are told:

> Remember Shabbat and keep her holy. Six days shall you work, but the seventh day is the Shabbat of *YHVH* your God: you shall do no work—neither you, your son or daughter, your male or female slaves, your livestock, or the

stranger who resides within your towns. For in six days *YHVH* made sky and earth and sea—and all that dwells in them—and then rested on the seventh day; therefore *YHVH* blessed Shabbat and set it apart.

(EXODUS 20:8–11)

When Moses recounts the Ten Sayings in the book of Deuteronomy, he remembers them with a slight but not insignificant change in the text:

Observe Shabbat and keep her holy, as *YHVH* your God commanded you. Six days shall you work, but the seventh day is the Shabbat of *YHVH* your God: you shall do no work—neither you, your son or daughter, your male or female slaves, your oxen or donkeys or any of your livestock, or the stranger who resides within your settlements, so that even your male and female slaves may rest as well as you. Remember that you were slaves in the land of Egypt, and *YHVH* your God brought you out from there with a mighty hand and an extended arm. For this reason *YHVH* commanded you to observe Shabbat.

(DEUTERONOMY 5:12–15)

In the book of Exodus, the rationale for Shabbat is linked to creation: God rested on the seventh day, and somehow God's rest mandates that you do the same. There is no intrinsic logic in this, but we can assume that since humans are created in the image of God, we create as God creates, and thus we must rest as God must rest.

In Deuteronomy, the logic is clearer: Shabbat is a mnemonic device recalling the Exodus from Egypt, rather than the creation of the universe. We are to keep the Sabbath and extend rest to all beings because doing so reminds us of our slavery and God's liberating us from that slavery, and, by extension, our charge to liberate others as well.

But what does any of this have to do with grace? To answer this question let's recall our definition of grace: Grace is *God's unlimited, unconditional, unconditioned, and all-inclusive love for all creation.* Grace is not earned or merited; it is simply given and, if you are attuned to God the way a radio is tuned to a broadcast, received.

Shabbat as a Day of Receiving

As we saw in chapter 2, creation itself is a manifestation of God's grace. Shabbat is the capstone of creation: labor isn't endless but is capped by rest. The six days of creation and the seventh day of rest go together like all the other opposites that God manifests. The quality of your work isn't at issue: you don't get to make Shabbat only if the quality of your labor merits it. On the contrary, you get to rest from work regardless of how hard or well you worked. In fact, working isn't even a prerequisite for Shabbat:

the seventh day comes with the same regularity and unconditionality as the other days of the week. You don't earn Shabbat, you receive it.

The emphasis on receiving is made clear in the very name given to the Jewish liturgy that opens Shabbat: *Kabbalat Shabbat,* "Receiving Shabbat." Receiving the Sabbath is the ideal human response to God's giving of Shabbat. I can throw a football to you, but you still have to choose to catch it. My throwing may be an act of unmerited grace, but your receiving the tossed ball requires you to take action. This is the paradox of Shabbat: the nonaction of Shabbat requires action, the act of receiving. We have seen this before. God creates us with the capacity to live free, to live graciously. God gives us the Ten Sayings as guidelines for doing so. But it is up to us whether or not to use them. The gift is freely given. Unwrapping and receiving it are a matter of choice.

The opening hymn of *Kabbalat Shabbat* is Psalm 95, *L'chu N'rananah:* "Come, Let Us Sing [to *YHVH*]." In it we are told, "*[YHVH]* is our God and we God's pastured herds and shepherded sheep—even today!—if we would but hear God's call!" (Psalm 95:7). This text contains both an expression of grace: we are already God's flock; and an "if–then" proposition: we can know this only if we hear God's call.

As we have argued throughout this book, God nature is grace, unconditional love, expressed in this poem as the act of shepherding. We don't merit God's grace (grace that must be earned isn't true grace), there is nothing we need do to be shepherded by God, but if we are to realize God's shepherding grace, we must hear God's call. According to Psalm 95, then, listening is the key to accepting the freely offered grace of God.

To Listen and to Love

Why is listening the key? What is it about listening that links it to grace? To answer this let's take a look at two other biblical texts central to Jewish liturgy, the *Shema* and the *Ve'ahavta,* "To Listen and to Love":

Hear, O Israel, *YHVH* is our God, *YHVH* is one. You shall love *YHVH* with a whole heart, with every breath, with all you have and are.

(DEUTERONOMY 6:4–5)

Given that *YHVH* is the is- *ing* of the life, we might understand the text this way:

Israel, listen to the divine happening within and around you, and when you listen, you will love reality with a whole heart, with every breath, with all you have and are.

While volumes have and can yet be written about the meaning of the *Shema* and the *Ve'ahavta,* what matters to us here is the link between listening and loving. Torah isn't commanding us to love, for love cannot be commanded. Rather, it is pointing out that if we listen deeply, we will be filled with love. Don't read "Hear, O Israel" and "You shall love" as commands, but as an axiom: "If you listen, you will love."

Linking listening and love shouldn't surprise you. You learn the connection between the two from the people you love all the time. Your friends, your children, your spouse or partner, what do they want most from you? They want you to listen to them. Listening says you care; listening says the other is important to you; listening says you will make the time and the effort to be present to another's pain and joy; listening says, I love you.

Listening is how we receive love. It is also one way to receive the Shabbat and the grace she offers. With this in mind we might even say that making time for listening is what a grace-filled Shabbat is all about.

Be careful not to imagine that listening can be ritualized or that it is the same from one Shabbat to the next. Listening is new every time it is done, for you never know what it is you are going to hear and how it is you are going to respond (if response is necessary). Listening is a creative act, and because it is, I have been told that it is antithetical to Shabbat. We are not supposed to create on Shabbat. But being creative and creating are not the same thing. The latter focuses on the ends, the former on the means. Focusing on the ends, the product being created, makes this kind of creativity work. Focusing on the means, the process, makes it play. A grace-filled Shabbat is always about play and never about work.

When we focus on the result, we seek to control outcomes, that is, we seek to impose our will on whatever or whomever we are working with to ensure that the result of our interaction matches the outcome we imagined. Controlling outcomes and imposing our will is at the heart of work, but not of genuine play, something done *lishmah,* for the sheer joy of doing it.

To understand this better, imagine a young woman playing soccer for her high school team. Her focus is on winning. When she furthers that end, she is happy; when she doesn't, she is frustrated, angry, and self-recriminating. Now compare this to her four-year-old cousin who is kicking a soccer ball around just for the joy of it. The toddler doesn't care about winning or losing. She simply delights in running and kicking. The older cousin is engaged in work; her younger cousin is engaged in play. The older knows success and failure, happiness and despair; the younger knows pure joy. Making Shabbat a day of grace is playing with pure joy.

Sing a New Song

Psalm 96, the second of the Shabbat psalms, tells us to "sing a new song to God" (Psalm 96:1). Singing a *new* song is an act of creativity whose focus is on means rather than ends, play rather than work. A new song isn't simply one you wrote last week and sing for the first time on Shabbat. A new song is one that flows out of you in the midst of Shabbat play. If you sit down on a Saturday to compose a new song, this is work. If you simply surrender yourself to Shabbat the way you might surrender yourself to a warm shower, the song may simply arise as a gift of grace. To sing a new song is to sing what arises in the playfulness of Shabbat.

And once sung, this new song is no longer new, so the following Shabbat you need sing yet another new song. Shabbat is a time for listening to what arises spontaneously within the context of Shabbat play and then giving it voice. This is hearing the call of God; this is listening to the presence of God within you. The focus on singing a new song prevents you from making a fetish of the old songs. It prevents you from making last Shabbat a mold for every subsequent Shabbat. It prevents you from working to conform to some ideal rather than surrendering to the play that is grace.

Go back to the creation of Shabbat in Genesis. God labors for six days, and on each day God does something that had not been done previously. Before the first day there was no light, before the third day there was no sun or moon, before the sixth day there were no people, before the seventh day there was no Shabbat. If we are to make Shabbat for ourselves, we must do so as God did in the beginning: not by imitating what had gone before but by doing something unprecedented, something new. Shabbat is no less creative than the workdays, only creative in a different way.

Listen carefully to the *Kiddush* for Sabbath eve, the blessing recited before drinking wine on Shabbat:

The sixth day. And the earth and sky and all within them were complete. On the seventh day God completed all the work of creation, and God did nothing on the seventh day that had already been done. God blessed the seventh day and hallowed it, because on it God did nothing that God had done before.

It isn't that there is no creativity on the seventh day; it is that the seventh day itself is creative. All the other days of the week were vessels for something else; Shabbat is a vessel only for itself. Making Shabbat—doing nothing that you have done before—is living the grace of God. With regard to listening, it must be done for its own sake: not to earn another's favor, but simply as an act of grace. And when it is so done, love arises.

Of course I'm not describing Shabbat as she has come to be defined by Rabbinic law and Jewish custom. I'm not talking about abstaining from driving cars, using electricity, and walking more than 2000 cubits (0.596 mile). You can follow as many or as few of the traditional Shabbat prohibitions as you wish. I am talking about Shabbat grace; the grace that is Shabbat; the free-flowing unconditioned love of God manifest in a day when you do what you have not done before. And because you have not done it before, you cannot know what it is in advance.

This is your new song, one not yet sung and certainly not yet composed. Shabbat as grace is a day of surprise, improvisation, and serendipity. And what happens if you fail to make such a day for yourself? You die.

> One who violates Shabbat shall be put to death: whoever works on it shall be cut off from the people.

> (EXODUS 31:14)

Well, which is it: will the Sabbath violator be executed or shunned? If we take the notion of being put to death literally, there is no point in following up this punishment with shunning or exile. After all, you're dead, so what difference does it make to you? If we are to reconcile the two punishments, we must take the first metaphorically: if you fail to set aside one day a week for freedom, for singing a new song, for listening and loving, you will be as one who is dead.

Since so much of our Sabbath liturgy refers to singing, think in terms of music. Without the rest between notes, a composition is merely noise. Without Shabbat to punctuate the work of the other six days, your life is merely noise. Living without Shabbat is living contingent on work. Living without Shabbat is earning a living rather than living your life. And if you imagine life must be earned before it can be lived, you have hardened your heart against receiving the grace of God: life itself.

Sex, Sunshine, and Shabbat: Tasting the World to Come

In the Talmud *(Berachot* 57b) the Rabbis tell us that there are three experiences in this world that give us a taste of *Olam haBa,* the World to Come: Shabbat, sexual orgasm, and a sunny day. What do these three have in common?

Of the three, Shabbat is the least corporeal, so let's work with orgasm and a sunny day first and then extrapolate from these what is meant by Shabbat as a link to *Olam haBa.* What might a sunny day and orgasm have in common? My guess is this: they are both acts of receptivity. If this is true, this is what a sunny day and orgasm have in common with Shabbat: all three require a cessation of activity in a moment of blissful receptivity.

Of course if we make cessation of activity an activity in itself, we cannot receive the bliss the moment offers. We have to slip from a state of doing to a state of nondoing, and do so without doing anything at all. The paradox, I hope, is self-evident: you cannot make not working and nondoing into another type of working and doing, though Rabbinic law regarding Shabbat may lead you to think otherwise. Again, this is where grace enters the picture.

You can work for six days, but you cannot work for Shabbat. You can work to draw close to sexual union, but the ecstasy of that union is a gift. You can take yourself outside and step into the sunshine, but the moment of basking in the warmth and the light is not your doing, only your receiving. Receiving on your part, just like the giving on God's part, is grace.

Now let's link this to *Olam haBa,* the World to Come. Without getting lost in a debate over whether or not such a world exists, and whether it exists in space (a World) and time (to Come), or whether it is a state of mind that can be received here and now, we can take from the teaching of the Rabbis the notion that whatever, whenever, and wherever *Olam haBa* may be, it is an experience of absolute receptivity; it is a state of perfect grace.

Grace, Shabbat, and Creation

Shabbat is a reminder of creation: "For in six days *YHVH* made sky, earth, and sea, and all that is contained in them, and on the seventh day God rested; therefore *YHVH* blessed the Sabbath day and made it holy" (Exodus 20:11). Creation is a gift of pure grace: life wasn't earned or deserved; after all, there was nothing and no one to earn and deserve it. Creation happened because it is the nature of God to create. It could not be otherwise. God is necessarily God, and to be God is to create. Creation and grace are inexorably linked.

Shabbat, being the capstone of creation, is no less linked to creation and grace. Despite the Torah's wording, can we really imagine God as needing to rest? While our liturgy tells us that God *shavat vayinafash,* God sat down and took a breather, few of us take this literally. Rather than imagine God as a worker on a break, imagine a composer parsing notes with rests. If we think of creation as God's song, then both notes and rests, sound and silence are equal and integral parts of God's creativity. The workweek and Shabbat are both necessary; and because they are necessary, they are not earned; and because they are not earned but freely given, they are acts of divine grace.

And how are we to participate in this grace? Through receiving the gift that is given.

Grace, Shabbat, and Manna

If you want to know how to receive the gift of grace, I can think of no better way than to observe and imitate the way of manna. In Exodus we learn that God covered the wilderness with a delicate flaky substance that the people could eat. The Hebrews had never seen such a thing and they asked one another, *"Man hu?* What is this?" (Exodus 16:15). What it is, Moses tells them, is the bread *(lechem)* given to the Hebrews by God that they might eat and not starve. The word "manna" comes from the question *"Man hu?"*

God then commands the people to gather manna for each member of their household. The proper amount is one *omer* (four liters) per person. Those who gathered more discovered on returning to their tents that the extra manna they took was gone and they had exactly one *omer* per person left; those who gathered less discovered that their manna had increased to exactly one *omer* per person.

This too is an act of grace. More than that, it is a hint of the way grace works: each person receives exactly the same amount. If grace could be earned, then some would earn more and some would earn less, but earning has nothing to do with grace, which is why all are graced equally.

After the people had gathered the manna, Moses said to them, "Don't save any until morning" (Exodus 16:19). They were to gather in a day's worth of manna and consume it that day. Nothing was to be left over. Of course, people being people, some did put a bit of manna aside for the next day, and when they awoke the next morning they found their "leftovers" teeming with worms and maggots (Exodus 16:20).

The message here is simple: Grace cannot be hoarded. Grace cannot be saved or preserved. Grace is for this moment, and when the moment passes so does the grace, replaced by the grace of the next moment. This is why we are told that while the people could gather manna each morning, by midafternoon, the hottest time of the day, "it melted" (Exodus

16:21). But there is more to this story than the fact that manna doesn't hold up well under desert heat.

Imagine yourself to be among the Hebrews wandering in Sinai. Each morning you gather in the day's manna, eating it all by 3:00p.m. or so, and waiting until dawn to eat again. Chances are you've tested the staying power of manna, hoping to save a bit for dinner or maybe a late-night snack. But whatever you sought to preserve melted, and you only succeeded in eating less than you could when you could. By midweek you have learned how this manna thing works, and you have given yourself over to the rhythm of God's grace. But Shabbat is coming, and you are not allowed to gather manna on Saturday. If Friday's supply melts by 3:00p.m., are you and your family going to go hungry until Sunday morning? Not at all. All of a sudden, the rules change!

This is the nature of grace: it follows no rules. How could it? If there are rules, grace is no longer grace but a prize to be grasped by playing the game and following the rules. But there are no rules you can rely on when it comes to grace. You thought there were: there were the rules of Sunday, Monday, Tuesday and the rest—and then the rules change. But will you?

On Friday, Moses says to the Israelites, "This is what *YHVH* commands: Tomorrow is a day of complete nondoing, a holy rest for *YHVH*. Today take the manna and bake and boil it as you wish, and leave enough for tomorrow" (Exodus 16:23).

Leftovers? Tomorrow? No, no, this can't be right. We know the rules: eat what we will today and wait upon the grace of *YHVH* to feed us tomorrow. If we hoard it, the manna will rot. *YHVH* is calling you to trust beyond experience, beyond rules, for grace can come no other way. And the people did trust and they did keep leftovers and behold there were no worms and maggots! There was only manna, *man hu;* only what is! Of course there are always those who have to see for themselves, and some of the Hebrews did go out to gather fresh manna on Saturday, but there was none to be found (Exodus 16:27).

Nothing from Something

God is not happy with those who cannot trust, but God only complains; God does not punish them. God knows how difficult it is for us to live without the illusion of permanence. Rather than punish the untrusting, God (or Moses, the text is unclear) says to the people as a whole, "See, *YHVH* has given you Shabbat, and you can gather manna for two days on Friday so that you can stay where you are on Saturday and not leave your place on the seventh day" (Exodus 16:29).

In this passage, the key to receiving grace is staying where you are and keeping your place. Of course you might imagine that God is commanding the people not to move at all, or at least not to leave their tent, and there are those who do understand it this way and go to great lengths to create a loophole where none exists or is needed so that they may indeed leave their tents and homes on the Sabbath. But I want to stay with the text as given. Six days a week you can do what you must to collect your manna, but on the seventh day you can do nothing at all: the grace just comes. But while it comes to all, only some will be receptive to it: those who stay where they are and keep their place.

Imagine you are playing baseball and have taken up a position in right field. While rare, when a ball is hit and comes your way you have to run this way and that to get under it, but once you are under it you have to stay put and keep your place. You simply raise your glove and allow the ball to do what the ball was going to do all along: drop right into that place. You don't make the ball go where it goes; you only wait to receive it.

Now imagine that in the seventh inning the rules change: you are no longer allowed to run into position. The ball is hit, it is coming your way, and every bone and nerve ending in your body says, "Run! Move! Get under it!" But the rules have changed and you are commanded not to move. All you can do is watch as the ball does what it does and goes where it goes. And then—lo and behold—it comes to you where you are! Had you moved you would have missed it. This is the grace of the seventh inning, the grace of the seventh day, the grace of Shabbat.

For six days you shall go out and gather in, but on the Sabbath you shall not move but keep your place just where you are, and grace will come to you. This is called *ratzo vashov,* "running and returning," a phrase taken from Ezekiel 1:14, and used by Jewish mystics to speak of the shift from living life from the perspective of God's alter ego to living life from the perspective of your ego and back again. On Shabbat there is no *ratzo vashov,* no going out or gathering in; there is only being where you are. This is nondoing. This is receiving without earning. Every day you are graced by God, but receiving requires some effort, but on this day of effortlessness nondoing there is effortless receiving.

This is what makes grace so radical and Shabbat so difficult. We are trained to do, but you cannot train to not do, for the training itself is something. Unlike creation—something from nothing—Shabbat is nothing from something.

Staying Put

Of course Shabbat as prescribed by the Rabbis is filled with doing, even when much of it is disguised as nondoing. I make no judgment on any of this. However you keep the rules of Shabbat is up to you. You may imagine that the more rules you keep, the better Jew you are, or you may imagine that Shabbat needs to be adapted to the Jew rather than the Jew to Shabbat. I offer no opinion on this, for both are a leaving of one's place. Keeping the laws or breaking them, either way it is doing rather than nondoing that fills your Shabbat. I am not concerned with doing, with going out and gathering in. I am concerned with staying put and holding my place. So what does it mean to stay put and keep one's place?

Staying put refers to your body; keeping your place refers to your mind. The grace of Shabbat is received when we learn to sit still, physically and mentally. I'm not talking about sitting still from sundown Friday to sundown Saturday; that would be absurd. It would make of grace a test of endurance, and it is anything but. I am talking about an instant of being present: present in body and present in mind, and allowing the ball of grace of divine be- *ing* to drop into the glove of your be- *ing.*

Nor am I talking about adapting some yoga or meditation posture or making time for contemplation on Shabbat. This too is doing. I'm talking about non-doing, just being: being where you are physically and mentally. And where are you? Look! If you do, you will discover you are all over the place. You are distracted on every plane of being: physical, emotional, intellectual, and spiritual. There is no motionless center. There is no "true self" you can see distinct from the "false selves" of distracted ego. There is just going out and gathering in, *ratzo vashov.* That is who and what you are: a doing, a ceaseless going out and gathering in. Just see that.

Nothing to do differently, nothing to change, no one else to be—just observe your going out and gathering in over and over and over. Then notice, if only for an instant, that the observer isn't doing any of this. Of course, as soon as you observe this observer, it is no longer the observer but just another object of observation going out and gathering in. But it is possible to know in some way I will not pretend to define that you are greater than this going out and gathering in. You are the place in which all this happens, but the place itself doesn't go anywhere. This place is you. Not the going out you or the gathering in you, but a greater you, an all-embracing you that is, though you may not choose to admit it, none other than God.

The Place

The Hebrew word Torah uses when God tells us to not to leave our place on the seventh day is *makom.* It is the same word that the Rabbis come to use for God as well. In *Genesis Rabbah* 68:9, Rabbi Huna repeats the question asked of his teacher Rabbi Ami, "Why do the sages speak of God as *HaMakom,* The Place?" He then gives his teacher's answer to this question, "Because God is the place of the world, though the world is not the place of God." God is the field in which creation happens, and while creativity is the nature of God, no single manifestation of creation captures the whole of God.

When you take your place, you become aware that God is The Place and every place. This is what Jacob discovers when he awakes from his dream of the ladder linking earth and heaven and filled with angels rising and returning on it: "God is in this place [*makom*] and I, I didn't know it!" (Genesis 28:16). God is in this place because God is every place. And yes, we don't know it. Why? Because we, like Jacob's dream angels, are too busy racing up and down, going out and gathering in. It was only after Jacob observed the race of up and down, *ratzo vashov,* that he knew what the race distracts us from knowing: God is in this place as this place.

Shabbat is not the cessation of going out and gathering in, but the realization that the place all this is happening is God and you are in that place. I'm not saying this will stop the going out and gathering in; I am saying that changing what is isn't necessary. Changing what is violates the Sabbath. Being with what is, as mad and as exhausting as it is, is what constitutes Shabbat. And there is no doing here, only be- *ing.* And be- *ing* is the ultimate liberation.

Manna-tizing Shabbat

As we saw in Deuteronomy, Moses offers a slightly amended version of the Ten Sayings and links Shabbat not to creation but to liberation: "Remember that you were slaves in the land of Egypt, and *YHVH* your God brought you out from there with a mighty hand and an extended arm. For this reason *YHVH* commanded you to observe Shabbat" (Deuteronomy 5:15). No mention is made here of creation or the Sabbath's ties to it. Instead we are told not where the Sabbath comes from, but what it offers those who dare to keep their place and discover it as The Place: freedom.

Manna is grace, keeping one's place is grace, and now liberation is grace. But this liberation isn't only the historical Exodus from *Mitzrayim,* Egypt, but the ever-needed liberation from *m'tzarim,* the narrow places of our lives. Egypt is both a state and a state of mind. It is the place in which we are trapped. It is the conditioning that God urges us to abandon when God commands us through Abram to *lech lecha,* to walk *(lech)* inward *(lecha)* and leave behind the conditioning of country, culture, and kin (Genesis 12:1) that we might be led to that land God wishes us to inhabit.

Grace is freeing because it isn't about doing. Grace is liberating because it requires nothing of doing and everything of nondoing. And this grace is Shabbat grace, the grace of staying in one's place. To know your place as The Place is to be liberated from everything you are conditioned to do to achieve whatever it is you are conditioned to desire. Knowing that God is The Place that is your place here and now puts an end to religion, politics, economics, psychological growth, and every other system that insists you need to be other and elsewhere than you are. Knowing God as The Place, and hence This Place and Every Place, frees you to observe *ratzo vashov* without getting trapped in all the running and returning. Grace reveals the greater unity of being and becoming, eternity and time, now and then. Grace is all of it. And Shabbat is the one day a week when, if you keep your place, you are apt to discover it.

Shabbat grace is knowing that God is in this place, your place, every place. It is a knowing that liberates you from the bondage of having to do and the bondage of having not to do. Going out and gathering in are still in this place, nothing need change, but you are no longer limited by it or to it. You are free to go and not go, to gather and not gather. You are free from rules and the absence of rules. You are free to do and not do. And when you are free from all this, you cannot help but cease all your work and just play.

Conclusion

Life as It Is

Choose Life

God is the is-ing of infinite possibility. Grace is the is-ing of actualized reality in the present moment. Sometimes what is pleases you, sometimes it displeases you, but it is always grace. To paraphrase Deuteronomy 30:19, Behold, I place before you life and death, blessing and curse; now live what is given.

But how? How do we live what is, how do we meet God's grace, especially when that grace violates our deepest hopes, dreams, and desires? I have suggested that Job is our guide in this and that his radical acceptance of "the good and the bad from God" is all we can do. And I have suggested that Shabbat is the day we Jews set aside for living the Way of Job. But I fear that some will mistake radical acceptance for passivity, and this is not what I mean at all.

While Deuteronomy tells us that God places before us life and death, blessing and curse, God also challenges us to choose life. Again this doesn't mean that one can choose life as opposed to death, or choose blessing rather than curse. It means that one can choose to live in the sense of choosing to live wisely with life and death and blessing and curse.

Chances are you know someone who, although alive, chooses not to live; and others, though dying, who live passionately. This is what God calls us to do: live our living and live our dying "with all our heart, with every breath, with all we have and are." This is what it means to live God's grace with grace.

Notes

Introduction: What Is Grace?

[1] Yudit K. Greenberg, ed., *Encyclopedia of Love in World Religions* (Santa Barbara: ABC-CLIO, 2008), 268.

[2] Lawrence Hoffman, ed., *My People's Prayer Book: Traditional Prayers, Modern Commentaries,* vol.9, *Welcoming the Night: Minchah and Ma'ariv* (Woodstock, VT: Jewish Lights, 2005), 169.

Chapter 1: Grace & God

[1] Rabbi Moshe Cordovero, *Eilima Rabati,* fol.25a. (Lvov, 1881).

[2] Rabbi Schneur Zalman, *Likkutei Torah, Shir haShirim,* vol.41a (Brooklyn: Kehot Publication Society, 1979).

[3] Rabbi Menachem Mendel Schneerson, *Toward a Meaningful Life,* ed. Simon Jacobson (New York: William Morrow, 1995), 215.

[4] Baal Shem Tov, cited in Aryeh Kaplan, trans., *The Light Beyond: Adventures in Hassidic Thought* (New York: Moznaim, 1981), 37.

[5] Sfat Emet, *Otzar Ma'anarim u'Michtavim,* 75.f, cited in Arthur Green, *Ehyeh: A Kabbalah for Tomorrow* (Woodstock, VT: Jewish Lights, 1993), 22–23.

[6] *Shenei Luchot HaBrit, Shavuot,* 189b.

198

[7]   Menahem Nahum of Chernobyl, *Upright Practices, the Light of the Eyes,* trans. Arthur Green (Mahwah, NJ: Paulist Press, 1982), 100.

[8]   Ibid., 224.

[9]   *Likkutim Yekarim,* 115b, in Miles Krassen, *Uniter of Heaven and Earth* (New York: SUNY, 1998), 86.

[10] A. Cohen, *Everyman's Talmud* (New York: E.P. Dutton, 1949), 17.

[11] Solomon Schechter, *Aspects of Rabbinic Theology* (Woodstock, VT: Jewish Lights, 2009), 15.

[12] Ibid., 61.

[13] Abraham Joshua Heschel, *God in Search of Man: A Philosophy of Judaism* (New York: Jewish Publication Society, 1956), n16, 53.

[14] Ibid., 121.

Chapter 2: Grace & Creation

[1]   Maimonides, *The Guide of the Perplexed* 3:53, vol.2, trans. Shlomo Pines (Chicago: University of Chicago, 1963), 630.

[2]   Ibid., 630–31.

[3]   Ibid., vol.1, lxxii.

[4]   Ibid., vol.2, 524.

[5]   Ibid., vol.1, 125.

[6]   Ibid., 125.

[7]   Kenneth Seeskin, *Maimonides on the Origin of the World* (New York: Cambridge Press, 2005), 8.

[8]   Ibid.

[9]   Maimonides, *Guide of the Perplexed,* vol.2, 349–50.

[10] Ibid., 349.

[11] Ibid., 451.

[12] Leon Roth, *Spinoza, Descartes, and Maimonides* (New York: Russell & Russell, 1963), 107.

[13] Baruch Spinoza, *Ethics,* part I P29, in *The Collected Works of Spinoza,* vol.1, trans. Edwin M. Curley (Princeton: Princeton University Press, 1985), 29.

[14] Baruch Spinoza, *Ethics,* part IV, preface, in *Complete Works,* trans. Samuel Shirley (Indianapolis: Hackett Publishing Company, 2002), 321.

[15] Ibid., part I, appendix, 238.

[16] Nissan Dovid Dubov, *The Key to Kabbalah* (Brooklyn: Dwelling Place Publishing, 2006), online edition www.chabad.org/library/articl e_cdo/aid/361898/jewish/The-Purpose-of-C reation.htm.

[17] Schnuer Zalman, cited in *Tanya, the Masterpiece of Hasidic Wisdom: Selections Annotated and Explained,* trans. Rabbi Rami Shapiro (Woodstock, VT: SkyLight Paths, 2010), 113.

[18] Rabbi Levi Yitzchak, *Kedushat Levi,* trans. Eliyahu Munk (Brooklyn: Lambda Publishers, 2009), 1.

Chapter 3: Grace & Humanity

[1] Rami Shapiro, *Proverbs: Annotated and Explained* (Woodstock, VT: SkyLight Paths, 2010), 55.

[2] Samson Raphael Hirsch, *The Pentateuch,* vol.1 (Gateshead, UK: Judaica Press, 1999), 30.

[3] Irving B. Weiner and Donald K. Freedheim, *Handbook of Psychology* (Hoboken, NJ: John Wiley and Sons, 2003), 262.

[4] Hirsch, *Pentateuch,* 31.

[5] Ibid.

[6] Ibid.

[7] Ibid., 31–32.

[8] Rabbi Levi Yitzchak, *Kedushat Levi,* trans. Eliyahu Munk (Brooklyn: Lambda Publishers, 2009), 8.

Chapter 4: Grace & Covenant

[1] Samson Raphael Hirsch, *The Pentateuch,* vol.1 (Gateshead, UK: Judaica Press, 1999), 181.

[2] Ibid., 181–82.

[3] Baruch Spinoza, *Ethics,* trans. R.H.M. Elwes (St. Peter Port, UK: Dodo Press, 2009), 67.

Chapter 5: Grace & Forgiveness

[1] "Die Juden sind schuld!" in *Das eherne Herz,* trans. Randall Bytwerk (Munich: Zentralverlag der NSDAP, 1943), 85–91.

[2] Shmuel Yosef Agnon, *Days of Awe: A Treasury of Jewish Wisdom for Reflection, Repentance,*

and Renewal on the High Holy Days (New York: Schocken Books, 1995), 276–77.

Chapter 6: Grace & Faith

[1] David R. Blumenthal, *The Place of Faith and Grace in Judaism* (Austin, TX: Center for Judaic-Christian Studies, 1985), 25.
[2] Ibid., 26.
[3] Stephen Mitchell, *Book of Job* (San Francisco: North Point Press, 1987), 88.
[4] Ibid., 129.

Chapter 7: Grace & the Ten Sayings

[1] Rabbi Levi Yitzchak, *Kedushat Levi,* trans. Eliyahu Munk (Brooklyn: Lambda Publishers, 2009), 9.
[2] I am indebted to the biblical scholar Jean-Yves Leloup for the notion of recasting the Ten Sayings in the positive. See his *Gospel of Mary Magdalene* (Rochester, VT: Inner Traditions International, 2002), 84.
[3] Huston Smith, *The World's Religions* (New York: HarperCollins, 1958), 287.

Suggestions for Further Reading

Agnon, Shmuel Yosef. *Days of Awe: A Treasury of Jewish Wisdom for Reflection, Repentance, and Renewal on the High Holy Days.* New York: Schocken Books, 1995.

Burrell, David. *Knowing the Unknowable God: Ibn Sina, Maimonides, Aquinas.* Notre Dame, IN: University of Notre Dame Press, 1986.

Cohen, A. *Everyman's Talmud.* New York: E.P. Dutton, 1949.

Dubov, Nissan Dovid. *The Key to Kabbalah.* Brooklyn: Dwelling Place Publishing, 2006.

Eisenbaum, Pamela. *Paul Was Not a Christian.* New York: HarperOne, 2009.

Fraenkel, Carlos. "Maimonides' God and Spinoza's *Deus sive Natura.*" *Journal of the History of Philosophy* 44, no.2 (2006):169–215.

Gillman, Neil. *The Death of Death: Resurrection and Immortality in Jewish Thought.* Woodstock, VT: Jewish Lights, 2006.

_____. *Doing Jewish Theology: God, Torah, & Israel in Modern Judaism.* Woodstock, VT: Jewish Lights, 2010.

_____. *Encountering God in Judaism.* Woodstock, VT: Jewish Lights, 2004.

_____. *Traces of God: Seeing God in Torah, History, and Everyday Life.* Woodstock, VT: Jewish Lights, 2006.

Ginsberg, H.L. *The Five Megilloth and Jonah.* Philadelphia: Jewish Publication Society, 1982.

Goldstein, Elyse. *New Jewish Feminism: Probing the Past, Forging the Future.* Woodstock, VT: Jewish Lights, 2009.

_____, ed. *Women's Torah Commentary.* Woodstock, VT: Jewish Lights, 2008.

Goodman, Lenn Even. *Rambam: Readings in the Philosophy of Moses Maimonides.* New York: Schocken Books, 1977.

Green, Arthur. *Ehyeh: A Kabbalah for Tomorrow.* Woodstock, VT: Jewish Lights, 1993.

204

_____, trans. *Menahem Nahum of Chernobyl: Upright Practices, the Light of the Eyes.* Mahwah, NJ: Paulist Press, 1982.

Greenberg, Yudit K., ed. *Encyclopedia of Love in World Religions.* Santa Barbara: ABC-CLIO, 2008.

Hartman, David. *A Living Covenant: The Innovative Spirit in Traditional Judaism.* Woodstock, VT: Jewish Lights Publishing, 2010.

Heschel, Abraham Joshua. *God in Search of Man: A Philosophy of Judaism.* New York: Jewish Publication Society, 1956.

Hirsch, Samson Raphael. *The Pentateuch.* Gateshead, UK: Judaica Press, 1999.

Hoffman, Lawrence, ed. *My People's Prayer Book: Traditional Prayers, Modern Commentary,* vol.9, *Welcoming the Night: Minchah and Ma'ariv* Woodstock, VT: Jewish Lights, 2005.

Kaplan, Aryeh, trans. *The Light Beyond: Adventures in Hassidic Thought.* New York: Moznaim, 1981.

Korn, Eugene. "Legal Floors and Moral Ceilings: A Jewish Understanding of Law and Ethics." *Edah Journal* 2:2.

Krassen, Miles. *Uniter of Heaven and Earth.* New York: SUNY, 1998.

Kushner, Lawrence. *God was in this Place & I, I did not know.* Woodstock, VT: Jewish Lights, 2006.

_____. *Honey from the Rock.* Woodstock, VT: Jewish Lights, 2005.

_____. *I'm God; You're Not: Observations on Organized Religion & Other Disguises of the Ego.* Woodstock, VT: Jewish Lights, 2010.

_____. *The River of Light.* Woodstock, VT: Jewish Lights, 2000.

Leloup, Jean-Yves. *Gospel of Mary Magdalene.* Rochester, VT: Inner Traditions International, 2002.

Levi Yitzchak. *Kedushat Levi.* Translated by Eliyahu Munk. Brooklyn: Lambda Publishers, 2009.

Maimonides, Moses. *The Guide of the Perplexed.* Translated by Shlomo Pines. Chicago: University of Chicago Press, 1974.

Mason, Richard. *The God of Spinoza.* Cambridge: Cambridge University Press, 2001.

Matt, Daniel. *Zohar: Annotated and Explained.* Woodstock, VT: SkyLight Paths, 2009.

Michaelson, Jay. *Everything Is God: The Radical Path of Nondual Judaism.* Boston: Shambhala/Trumpeter, 2009.

Mitchell, Stephen. *The Book of Job.* San Francisco: North Point Press, 1987.

Montefiore, C.G. *A Rabbinic Anthology.* New York: Schocken Books, 1974.

Philo. *The Works of Philo.* Translated by C.D. Yonge. Peabody, MA: Hendrickson Publishers, 2008.

Rosenblatt, Samuel. *High Ways to Perfection of Abraham Maimonides.* New York: AMS Press, 1966.

Roth, Leon. *Spinoza, Descartes, and Maimonides.* New York: Russell & Russell, 1963.

Roth, Norman. *Maimonides: Essays and Texts, 850th Anniversary.* Madison: Hispanic Seminary of Medieval Studies, 1985.

Sanders, E.P. *Paul and Palestinian Judaism.* Philadelphia: Fortress Press, 1977.

Schechter, Solomon. *Aspects of Rabbinic Theology.* Woodstock, VT: Jewish Lights, 2009.

Schnuer Zalman. *Likutei Amarim Tanya.* Bilingual edition. Brooklyn: Kehot Publication Society, 1998.

Seeskin, Kenneth. *Maimonides on the Origin of the World.* New York: Cambridge Press, 2005.

Shapiro, Rami. *Divine Feminine in Biblical Wisdom Literature.* Woodstock, VT: SkyLight Paths, 2005.

_____. *Proverbs: Annotated and Explained.* Woodstock, VT: Skylight Paths, 2011.

_____. *Tanya, the Masterpiece of Hasidic Wisdom: Selections Annotated and Explained.* Woodstock, VT: Skylight Paths, 2010.

Singer, Isadore. *The Jewish Encyclopedia.* Jersey City, NJ: KTAV Publishing, 1970.

Smith, Huston. *The World's Religions.* New York: HarperCollins, 1958.

Spinoza, Baruch. *The Book of God.* Edited by Dagobert Runes. New York: Philosophical Library, 1958.

_____. *The Collected Works of Spinoza.* vol.1. Translated by Edwin M. Curley. Princeton: Princeton University Press, 1985.

_____. *Complete Works.* Translated by Samuel Shirley. Indianapolis: Hackett Publishing Company, 2002.

_____. *Ethics.* Translated by R.H.M. Elwes. St Peter Port, UK: Dodo Press, 2009. New York: Schocken Books, 2002.

Strassfeld, Michael. *The Jewish Holidays.* New York: Harper & Row, 1985.

Weiner, Irving B., and Donald K. Freedheim. *Handbook of Psychology.* Hoboken, NJ: John Wiley and Sons, 2003.

Wienpahl, Paul. *The Radical Spinoza.* New York: New York University Press, 1979.

Yellin, David. *Maimonides.* Charleston, SC: Nabu Press, 2010.

Waskow, Arthur. *Seasons of Our Joy.* New York: Summit Books, 1982.

About the Author

Rabbi Rami Shapiro is a renowned teacher of spirituality across faith traditions, a noted theologian, and an award-winning storyteller, poet and essayist. He is a popular speaker on the topics of Judaism, theology and spirituality. See the Also Available section for other Jewish Lights/SkyLight Paths books by him.

Looking for an inspirational speaker for an upcoming event, Shabbaton or retreat?

Jewish Lights authors are available to speak and teach on a variety of topics that educate and inspire. For more information about our authors who are available to speak to your group, visit www.jewishlights.com/page/category/JLSB. To book an event, contact the Jewish Lights Speakers Bureau at publicity@jewishlights.com or call us at (802)457-4000.

Also Available from Rabbi Rami Shapiro

The Sacred Art of Lovingkindness:
Preparing to Practice

by Rabbi Rami Shapiro

Explores Judaism's Thirteen Attributes of Lovingkindness as the framework for cultivating a life of goodness.

The Divine Feminine in Biblical Wisdom Literature:
Selections Annotated & Explained

212

Translation & Annotation by Rabbi Rami Shapiro

Foreword by Rev. Cynthia Bourgeault, PhD

Ecclesiastes:
Annotated & Explained

Translation and Annotation by Rabbi Rami Shapiro

Foreword by Rev. Barbara Cawthorne Crafton

Ethics of the Sages:
Pirke Avot—Annotated & Explained

Translation and Annotation by Rabbi Rami Shapiro

Hasidic Tales:
Annotated & Explained

Translation & Annotation by Rabbi Rami Shapiro

The Hebrew Prophets:
Selections Annotated & Explained

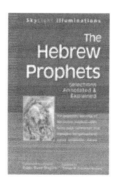

Translation & Annotation by Rabbi Rami Shapiro
Foreword by Zalman M. Schachter-Shalomi

Proverbs:
Annotated & Explained

Translation and Annotation by Rabbi Rami Shapiro

Tanya, the Masterpiece of Hasidic Wisdom:
Selections Annotated & Explained

Translation and Annotation by Rabbi Rami Shapiro

About Jewish Lights

People of all faiths and backgrounds yearn for books that attract, engage, educate, and spiritually inspire.

Our principal goal is to stimulate thought and help all people learn about who the Jewish People are, where they come from, and what the future can be made to hold. While people of our diverse Jewish heritage are the primary audience, our books speak to people in the Christian world as well and will broaden their understanding of Judaism and the roots of their own faith.

We bring to you authors who are at the forefront of spiritual thought and experience. While each has something different to say, they all say it in a voice that you can hear.

Our books are designed to welcome you and then to engage, stimulate, and inspire. We judge our success not only by whether or not our books are beautiful and commercially successful, but by whether or not they make a difference in your life.

For your information and convenience, at the back of this book we have provided a list of other Jewish Lights books you might find interesting and useful. They cover all the categories of your life:

Bar/Bat Mitzvah • Bible Study/Midrash • Children's Books • Congregation Resources • Current Events/History • Ecology/Environment • Fiction:

Mystery, Science Fiction • Grief/Healing • Holidays/Holy Days • Inspiration • Kabbalah/Mysticism/Enneagram • Life Cycle • Meditation • Men's Interest • Parenting • Prayer/Ritual/Sacred Practice • Social Justice • Spirituality • Theology/Philosophy • Travel • Twelve Steps • Women's Interest

Grace—God's unlimited, unconditional, unconditioned & all-inclusive love for all creation.

***

Jews often dismiss "grace" as a valid and vital aspect of Judaism. Yet without a sophisticated knowledge of grace as Judaism understands grace, Jews are robbed of an important component of our faith that leaves us with only a partial understanding of our tradition, our God and the life we are called to live.

Rabbi Rami Shapiro seeks to reclaim grace as a core Jewish idea, presenting it as a key for unlocking the spiritual nature of all aspects of Judaism. He examines elements of Judaism—God, creation, humanity, covenant, faith—in relation to grace. He highlights the role of grace in key aspects of Jewish practice, such as forgiveness, the Ten Sayings and Shabbat. In so doing, he will enrich your appreciation of grace in a Jewish context and deepen your appreciation of Judaism as a way of living graciously.

***

"Demonstrates with skill and textual insight how Judaism can reclaim grace as an unambiguous part of our covenant with an unconditionally loving and always present God. A must read for those seeking wisdom in sacred texts and practical methods to participate in a God-graced life."

—Rabbi David Lyon, Congregation Beth Israel, Houston, Texas; author, *God of Me: Imagining God throughout Your Lifetime*

"Rabbi Shapiro has done it again. Fans of Rabbi Rami's writing will be delighted by his in-depth exploration of chesed, approached with both erudition and grace."

—Rabbi Jamie S. Korngold, author, *The God Upgrade: Finding Your 21st-Century Spirituality in Judaism's 5,000-Year-Old Tradition*

Rabbi Rami Shapiro is a renowned teacher of spirituality across faith traditions, a noted theologian, and an award-winning storyteller, poet and essayist. He is a popular speaker on the topics of Judaism, theology and spirituality. See below for other Jewish Lights/SkyLight Paths books by him.

***

"An amazing case for amazing grace as a Jewish virtue. Only such agility of mind and facility of expression can breathe and breed the conviction that powers this therapeutic tour de force. Promises a startling shake-up for Jewish-Christian dialogue."

—**Rabbi Michael J. Cook,** Bronstein Professor of Judeo-Christian Studies, Hebrew Union College; author, *Modern Jews Engage the New Testament: Enhancing Jewish Well-Being in a Christian Environment*

"Don't be deceived! This is a radical book of Jewish theology, revisioning God, Torah and Israel in a way that may well blow your mind. Or open your heart. Or, hopefully, both."

—**Jay Michaelson,** author, *Everything Is God: The Radical Path of Nondual Judaism and God in Your Body: Kabbalah, Mindfulness and Embodied Spiritual Practice*

Also Available from Rabbi Rami Shapiro

The Sacred Art of Lovingkindness Preparing to Practice

By Rabbi Rami Shapiro

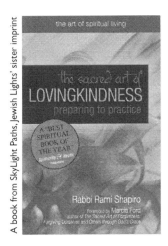

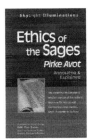

Explores Judaism's Thirteen Attributes of Lovingkindness as the framework for cultivating a life of goodness.

Back Cover Material

The question isn't whether grace is there for you in Judaism. The question is,
do you have the courage to accept it?

"Fascinating.... Does the important job of correcting mistaken impressions about Judaism and its relationship to *chesed* ... in the context of articulating [the author's] own unique theology. Rami Shapiro's voice is a significant one in the emerging world of American Jewish spirituality."

—Rabbi Arthur Green, author, *Seek My Face: A Jewish Mystical Theology.*

"For Rabbi Rami Shapiro, one of American Judaism's great teachers, all existence is flooded by divine *chesed* (or grace); here is another and higher way to love and be loved.... Offers us not only the blueprint for an evolved Jewish theology but one that also convincingly demonstrates the centrality of love in Jewish life and thought."

—Rabbi Lawrence Kushner, author, *I'm God, You're Not: Observations on Organized Religion & Other Disguises of the Ego*

"Powerful ... this thought-provoking book teaches us that abundance and goodness abound, and that through deed and practice Judaism provides an avenue to mindful and compassionate living."

—Rabbi Karyn D. Kedar, author, *God Whispers: Stories of the Soul, Lessons of the Heart*

> "*Chesed* isn't a reward; it is reality. God's grace isn't limited to what we want to happen or might like to happen. God's grace is what is happening whether we like it or not. In short, God's grace is the giving of all to all."
> **—FROM THE INTRODUCTION**

Ask almost any Jew whether grace is a central concept in Judaism and an essential element in living Jewishly and, chances are, their answer will be "no." But that's the wrong answer. This fascinating foray into God's love freely given offers you—regardless of your level of Jewish involvement—a way to answer that question in the affirmative.

Drawing from ancient and contemporary, traditional and non-traditional Jewish wisdom, this book reclaims the idea of grace in Judaism in three ways:

- It offers a view of God that helps you understand what grace is, why grace is, and how grace manifests in the world.

- It sets forth a reading of Judaism that is grace-filled: an understanding of creation, Shabbat and other Jewish practices from a grace-filled perspective.

- It challenges you to be embraced and transformed by grace, and to live life as a vehicle for God's grace, thereby fulfilling the promise of being created in God's image and likeness.

Books For ALL Kinds of Readers

At ReadHowYouWant we understand that one size does not fit all types of readers. Our innovative, patent pending technology allows us to design new formats to make reading easier and more enjoyable for you. This helps improve your speed of reading and your comprehension. Our EasyRead printed books have been optimized to improve word recognition, ease eye tracking by adjusting word and line spacing as well as minimizing hyphenation. Our EasyRead SuperLarge editions have been developed to make reading easier and more accessible for vision-impaired readers. We offer Braille and DAISY formats of our books and all popular E-Book formats.

We are continually introducing new formats based upon research and reader preferences. Visit our web-site to see all of our formats and learn how you can Personalize our books for yourself or as gifts. Sign up to Become A RHYW Registered Reader.

www.readhowyouwant.com

34776760R00137

Made in the USA
Middletown, DE
04 September 2016